Kathryn Slocombe

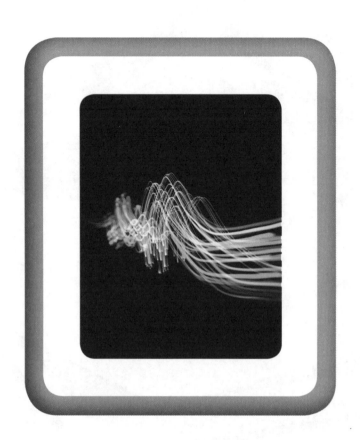

ESSENTIALS

GCSE AQA

Anthology: Character & Voice

Acknowledgements

The author and publisher are grateful for permission to use quoted materials:

p.4, 40, 46 'The Clown Punk' from *Tyrannosaurus Rex Versus the Corduroy Kid* (Faber, 2006), copyright © Simon Armitage 2006, reprinted by permission of Faber & Faber Ltd.

p.6–7, 46 *Checking Out Me History* copyright © 1996 by John Agard, reproduced by kind permission of John Agard c/o Caroline Sheldon Literary Agency Limited.

p.8–9, 46 'Horse Whisperer' by Andrew Forster, from *Fear of Thunder* (Flambard Press, 2007), reprinted by permission of the publisher.

p.10–11, 46 'Medusa' by Carol Ann Duffy from *The World's Wife* (Picador 2000), copyright © Carol Ann Duffy 2000, reprinted by permission of Pan Macmillan, London.

p.12–13 'Singh Song!' by Daljit Nagra, from *Look We Have Coming to Dover* (Faber, 2007), copyright © Daljit Nagra 2007, reprinted by permission of the publishers, Faber & Faber Ltd.

p.14, 46 'Brendon Gallacher' by Jackie Kay, from *Darling: New and Selected Poems* (Bloodaxe Books, 2007), reprinted by permission of Bloodaxe Books.

p.16, 40, 46 'Give' from *The Dead Sea Poems* (Faber, 2006), copyright © Simon Armitage 1995, reprinted by permission of Faber & Faber Ltd.

p.18, 46 'Les Grands Seigneurs' by Dorothy Molloy, from *Hare Soup* (Faber, 2004), copyright © Dorothy Molloy 2004, reprinted by permission of the publishers, Faber & Faber Ltd.

p.24, 36–37, 39, 47 'The River God' by Stevie Smith from *The Collected Poems of Stevie Smith*, © Stevie Smith 1972, reprinted with kind permission of the Estate of James MacGibbon.

p.26–27, 47 'The Hunchback in the Park' by Dylan Thomas, from *Collected Poems 1934–1952* (Dent, 1952), reprinted by permission of David Higham Associates.

p.30–31, 42–43 *Casehistory: Alison (head injury)* ©U.A. Fanthorpe, reproduced with kind permission of R.V. Bailey.

p.32–33, 42–43, 47 'On a Portrait of a Deaf Man', from *Collected Poems*, by John Betjeman © The Estate of John Betjeman 1955, 1958, 1962, 1964, 1968, 1970, 1979, 1981, 1982, 2001. Reproduced by permission of John Murray (Publishers).

Contents

The Clown Punk

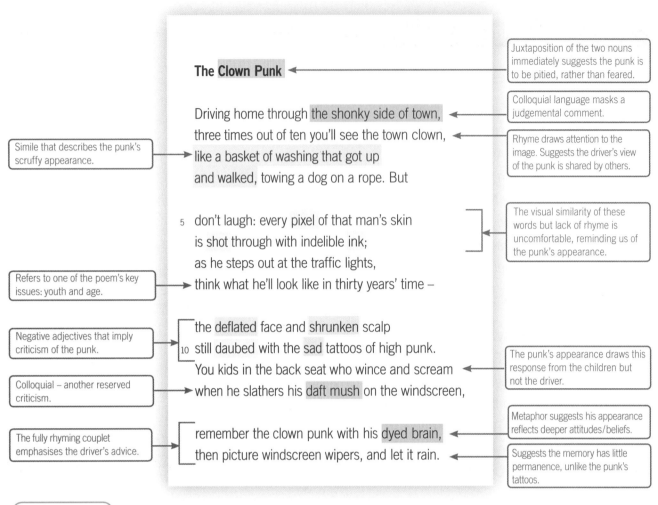

The Clown Punk

Driving home through the shonky side of town,
three times out of ten you'll see the town clown,
like a basket of washing that got up
and walked, towing a dog on a rope. But

5 don't laugh: every pixel of that man's skin
is shot through with indelible ink;
as he steps out at the traffic lights,
think what he'll look like in thirty years' time –

the deflated face and shrunken scalp
10 still daubed with the sad tattoos of high punk.
You kids in the back seat who wince and scream
when he slathers his daft mush on the windscreen,

remember the clown punk with his dyed brain,
then picture windscreen wipers, and let it rain.

Juxtaposition of the two nouns immediately suggests the punk is to be pitied, rather than feared.

Colloquial language masks a judgemental comment.

Rhyme draws attention to the image. Suggests the driver's view of the punk is shared by others.

Simile that describes the punk's scruffy appearance.

The visual similarity of these words but lack of rhyme is uncomfortable, reminding us of the punk's appearance.

Refers to one of the poem's key issues: youth and age.

Negative adjectives that imply criticism of the punk.

The punk's appearance draws this response from the children but not the driver.

Colloquial – another reserved criticism.

Metaphor suggests his appearance reflects deeper attitudes/beliefs.

The fully rhyming couplet emphasises the driver's advice.

Suggests the memory has little permanence, unlike the punk's tattoos.

Key Features

Juxtaposition	Colloquial language	Adjectives	Simile	Metaphor	Images/Art

Sonnet • Iambic pentameter • Philosophical

About the Poem

- Written by **Simon Armitage** (1963–).

- The poem describes a punk who is seen by a man and his children as they drive home through a run-down part of town. We hear the voice of the driver as he describes the punk to us.

- The punk's image and behaviour is intimidating, but the driver helps the children see it as a creation.

- As the punk is described, we also learn a little about the driver's attitudes and beliefs.

Ideas, Themes and Issues

- **Appearance:** The way we dress often influences how people see us. The punk's appearance reflects his beliefs and is intended to create a reaction.

- **Fear:** The children are afraid of the punk because of the way he looks and acts. The driver suggests this will change in time.

- **Youth:** The way we look, what we believe in, and what frightens us changes as we age.

- **Outsiders:** The clown punk is marginalised both metaphorically and physically.

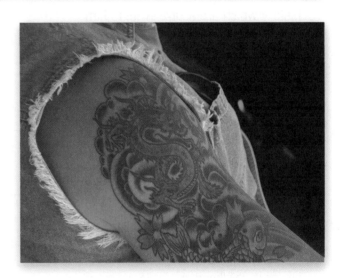

Form, Structure and Language

- The use of the **sonnet** form, which is typically associated with love poetry, could suggest a fondness for the punk.

- It has the same line structure as a traditional sonnet but both the **rhyme scheme** and **iambic pentameter** are disrupted, reflecting the punk's non-conformist appearance and attitudes.

- The reserved criticisms that the driver makes of the punk create a **philosophical** tone.

- The description of the punk in the third **stanza** suggests the driver pities him and wonders what his future holds.

- **Pathos** is created by the **juxtaposition** of the two **nouns** used in the title, 'Clown', 'Punk' and the **simile** in lines 3/4 that brings to mind the image of a shambolic looking figure.

- Words from the **semantic field** of **images/art** remind us that the punk's appearance is a creation.

Quick Test

1. What is the significance of the poem's title?
2. What is symbolic about the punk's position outside the car?
3. Which words in the third stanza suggest the narrator's pity for the punk?
4. What does 'indelible ink' mean, and which line offers a direct contrast to this image?

Checking Out Me History

About the Poem

- Written by **John Agard** (1949–).

- Through the poem we hear an Afro-Caribbean voice describing and reacting to what he has been taught in school.

- He mocks an education confined to the main events and people in British history which are as irrelevant to him as nursery rhymes.

- The achievements made by people from other cultures are missing from his education, leaving him struggling to understand his own history and identity.

- The poem ends with a decision to fill in these missing details.

Ideas, Themes and Issues

- **Personal identity**: Our sense of identity begins in childhood and is closely linked to our culture, history and language.

- **Colonialism**: When the British Empire colonised countries in the 19th and 20th centuries children were often educated in English and taught only British history.

- **History**: History is selective and is often written by the strongest side in any conflict. There are always two sides but often only one gets heard.

- **Rebellion**: The Caribbean figures in the poem had no power and were forced to rebel to change their situation, just as the voice in the poem has to.

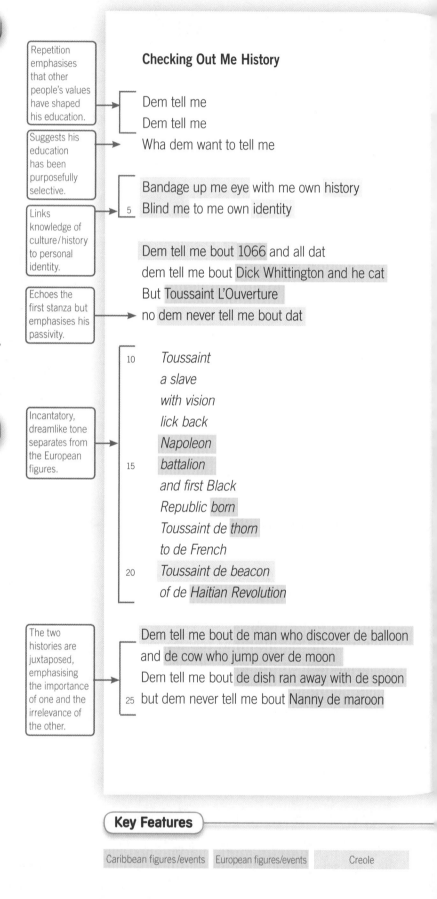

Checking Out Me History

Repetition emphasises that other people's values have shaped his education.

Dem tell me
Dem tell me

Suggests his education has been purposefully selective.

Wha dem want to tell me

Bandage up me eye with me own history
5 Blind me to me own identity

Links knowledge of culture/history to personal identity.

Dem tell me bout 1066 and all dat
dem tell me bout Dick Whittington and he cat
But Toussaint L'Ouverture

Echoes the first stanza but emphasises his passivity.

no dem never tell me bout dat

Incantatory, dreamlike tone separates from the European figures.

10   Toussaint
     a slave
     with vision
     lick back
     Napoleon
15   battalion
     and first Black
     Republic born
     Toussaint de thorn
     to de French
20   Toussaint de beacon
     of de Haitian Revolution

The two histories are juxtaposed, emphasising the importance of one and the irrelevance of the other.

Dem tell me bout de man who discover de balloon
and de cow who jump over de moon
Dem tell me bout de dish ran away with de spoon
25 but dem never tell me bout Nanny de maroon

Key Features

Caribbean figures/events   European figures/events   Creole

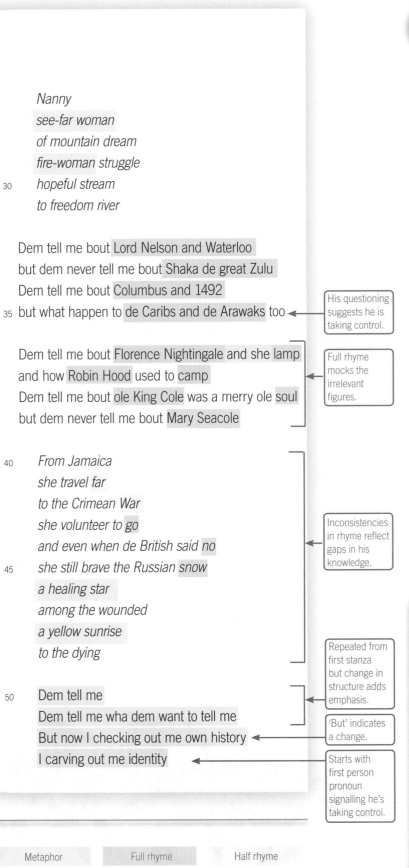

Nanny
see-far woman
of mountain dream
fire-woman struggle
30 hopeful stream
to freedom river

Dem tell me bout Lord Nelson and Waterloo
but dem never tell me bout Shaka de great Zulu
Dem tell me bout Columbus and 1492
35 but what happen to de Caribs and de Arawaks too

His questioning suggests he is taking control.

Dem tell me bout Florence Nightingale and she lamp
and how Robin Hood used to camp
Dem tell me bout ole King Cole was a merry ole soul
but dem never tell me bout Mary Seacole

Full rhyme mocks the irrelevant figures.

40 From Jamaica
she travel far
to the Crimean War
she volunteer to go
and even when de British said no
45 she still brave the Russian snow
a healing star
among the wounded
a yellow sunrise
to the dying

Inconsistencies in rhyme reflect gaps in his knowledge.

50 Dem tell me
Dem tell me wha dem want to tell me
But now I checking out me own history
I carving out me identity

Repeated from first stanza but change in structure adds emphasis.

'But' indicates a change.

Starts with first person pronoun signalling he's taking control.

Metaphor   Full rhyme   Half rhyme

Form, Structure and Language

- The **free verse** form, **lack of punctuation** and use of **Creole** in the poem could reflect the voice's refusal to use conventional English forms and **Standard English**.

- The tone is **mocking** in places but becomes increasingly **defiant** as the words 'dem tell me' are **repeated**.

- **Metaphors** linking the Caribbean figures to light are a contrast to the images of blindness that describe his **Eurocentric** education. These images create a link between understanding your own culture and the idea of **enlightenment**.

- **Inconsistent rhymes** and **half rhymes** reflect the voice's missing knowledge and feeling of incompleteness.

- The **shorter italicised lines** draw our attention to the significant historical figures. These lines sound **incantatory** as though the voice in the poem is calling them to life.

Quick Test

1. Why are there repeated references to nursery rhymes and folk tales?

2. What is significant about the metaphors used to describe the Caribbean figures?

3. How does the poet suggest that not knowing your own history is damaging?

4. What is significant about the last two lines of the poem?

Horse Whisperer

About the Poem

- Written by **Andrew Forster** (1964–).

- The poem tells the story of a horse whisperer – a person who soothes injured or distressed horses.

- The whisperer relates his story to us, telling us the secrets of his trade.

- His skills were once admired and sought-after, but changing times meant he was no longer needed and his methods were viewed with mistrust.

- The whisperer seeks revenge for the way he has been treated.

Ideas, Themes and Issues

- **Superstition / fear of the unknown**: The farmers and the church are afraid of the whisperer's charms and **talismans** as they don't know how they work.

- **Change and modernity**: Machinery replaces horses on the farms meaning there is less demand for the whisperer.

- **Revenge**: As revenge for being cast out of town, the whisperer uses his skills to unsettle the horses.

- **Outsiders**: The whisperer has always been outside society in a sense but he is further removed from it when he is forced to leave. There is a clear divide between society and the whisperer.

Horse Whisperer

> They shouted for me
> when their horses snorted, when restless
> hooves traced circles in the earth
> and shimmering muscles refused the plough.
> 5 My secret was a spongy tissue, pulled bloody
> from the mouth of a just-born foal,
> scented with rosemary, cinnamon,
> a charm to draw the tender giants
> to my hands.
>
> 10 They shouted for me
> when their horses reared at the burning straw
> and eyes revolved in stately heads.
> I would pull a frog's wishbone,
> tainted by meat, from a pouch,
> 15 a new fear to fight the fear of fire,
> so I could lead the horses,
> like helpless children, to safety.

Short, isolated opening line highlights disbelief at what has happened.

Language associated with secrecy, spells and magic. Compare this with lines 23 and 26.

Simile shows his tenderness towards the horses.

Key Features

Sensory details   Negative language   Admiration

Talisman • Free verse • Enjambment • Caesura

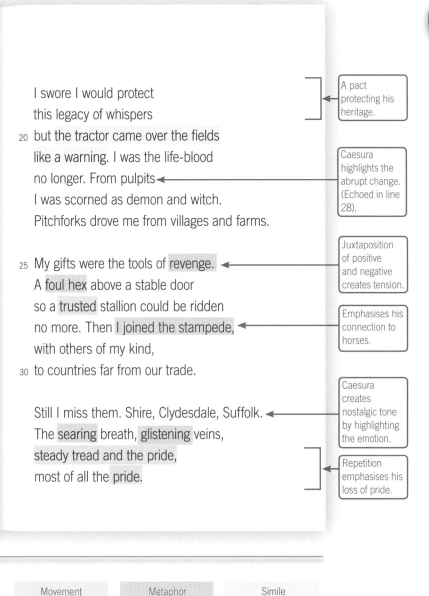

I swore I would protect
this legacy of whispers

[A pact protecting his heritage.]

20 but the tractor came over the fields
like a warning. I was the life-blood
no longer. From pulpits

[Caesura highlights the abrupt change. (Echoed in line 28).]

I was scorned as demon and witch.
Pitchforks drove me from villages and farms.

25 My gifts were the tools of revenge.

[Juxtaposition of positive and negative creates tension.]

A foul hex above a stable door
so a trusted stallion could be ridden
no more. Then I joined the stampede,

[Emphasises his connection to horses.]

with others of my kind,
30 to countries far from our trade.

Still I miss them. Shire, Clydesdale, Suffolk.

[Caesura creates nostalgic tone by highlighting the emotion.]

The searing breath, glistening veins,
steady tread and the pride,
most of all the pride.

[Repetition emphasises his loss of pride.]

Movement   Metaphor   Simile

Form, Structure and Language

- The **free verse** form and **enjambment** reflect the changes in the way the whisperer is seen. The **caesura** in line 22 echoes the abrupt turn in opinion about him.

- The **repeated line** that opens the first and second **stanzas** emphasises the fact that the need was on the farmers' side and shows how regularly the whisperer was summoned.

- The stanzas **become shorter** as the farmers have less need for his skills.

- **Sensory** details and words describing **movement** are used throughout the poem to create vivid descriptions.

- The **contrast** between the **admiring** descriptions of horses and the **negative language** used after he is cast out reveals the tension of the situation.

- At first the tone of the poem reflects the whisperer's **pride** in his skills. This turns to **anger** when he describes his betrayal, then to **nostalgia** in the final lines.

Quick Test

1. Apart from machinery, what other modern knowledge could have pushed whisperers out of the farms?

2. Which words show the whisperer's admiration for the horses and which provide a contrast?

3. How do we know that this experience is not unique to the whisperer whose voice we hear?

Medusa

About the Poem

- Written by **Carol Ann Duffy** (1955–).

- In this **dramatic monologue** we hear the voice of a woman who has become consumed with jealousy as she suspects her husband is being unfaithful.

- In an **extended metaphor** she is likened to the Greek mythical figure Medusa, whose head of snakes turned anyone who looked at her into stone. In the myth, Medusa's head of snakes was punishment for falling in love. Perseus killed Medusa as part of a quest.

- The woman's jealousy and battle with her husband is destructive, but she seems to relish the power she has, even though it will destroy her.

Ideas, Themes and Issues

- **Jealousy and possession**: The woman can't let go of her doubts about her husband but is determined to have him to herself, even if she destroys them both in the process.

- **Youth and beauty**: She describes how she was once beautiful and compares herself to her husband's 'girls'. In contrast, she now describes herself in negative terms.

- **Violence and love**: Her words have a threatening tone and her actions become increasingly violent. Her husband is linked to Perseus, foreshadowing her destruction.

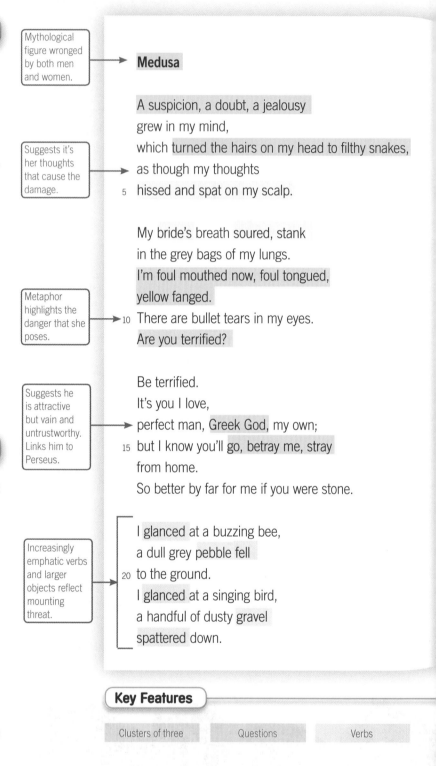

Mythological figure wronged by both men and women.

Medusa

A suspicion, a doubt, a jealousy
grew in my mind,
which turned the hairs on my head to filthy snakes,
as though my thoughts
5 hissed and spat on my scalp.

My bride's breath soured, stank
in the grey bags of my lungs.
I'm foul mouthed now, foul tongued,
yellow fanged.
10 There are bullet tears in my eyes.
Are you terrified?

Be terrified.
It's you I love,
perfect man, Greek God, my own;
15 but I know you'll go, betray me, stray
from home.
So better by far for me if you were stone.

I glanced at a buzzing bee,
a dull grey pebble fell
20 to the ground.
I glanced at a singing bird,
a handful of dusty gravel
spattered down.

Suggests it's her thoughts that cause the damage.

Metaphor highlights the danger that she poses.

Suggests he is attractive but vain and untrustworthy. Links him to Perseus.

Increasingly emphatic verbs and larger objects reflect mounting threat.

Key Features

Clusters of three   Questions   Verbs

Dramatic monologue • Extended metaphor • Free verse

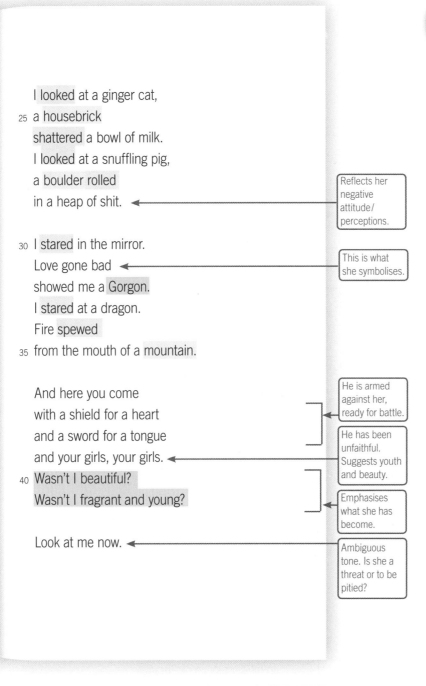

I looked at a ginger cat,
25 a housebrick
shattered a bowl of milk.
I looked at a snuffling pig,
a boulder rolled
in a heap of shit. ◄——— Reflects her negative attitude/ perceptions.

30 I stared in the mirror.
Love gone bad ◄——— This is what she symbolises.
showed me a Gorgon.
I stared at a dragon.
Fire spewed
35 from the mouth of a mountain.

And here you come ──── He is armed against her, ready for battle.
with a shield for a heart
and a sword for a tongue
and your girls, your girls. ◄─── He has been unfaithful. Suggests youth and beauty.
40 Wasn't I beautiful?
Wasn't I fragrant and young? ──── Emphasises what she has become.

Look at me now. ◄─── Ambiguous tone. Is she a threat or to be pitied?

Types of stone   Mythology   Sibilance

Form, Structure and Language

- Although this is a **free verse** poem, the **repetition**, **end rhyme** and **clusters of three** create a strong rhythm and link key ideas together.

- The tone is **unambiguous** from the first line with its **three negative emotions** and **sibilance** mimicking the hissing snakes.

- The question at the end of the second **stanza** and its echo in the next line create a **threatening tone** which continues as the woman uses her powers.

- The **verbs** become more **emphatic** and the objects she turns to stone become bigger reflecting an escalation in the threat she poses and her enjoyment of the power.

- **Pathos** is created through her **negative descriptions** of herself and the understanding that the man she loves will destroy her.

- The **ambiguity** of the last line, which is isolated from the rest of the poem, is threatening and may create **pathos** if taken as a desperate plea.

Quick Test

1. How are we encouraged to feel sympathy for the woman?

2. Explain the significance of the last line of the poem.

3. Why do you think she describes her husband as 'Greek God'?

Singh Song!

About the Poem

- Written by **Daljit Nagra** (1966–).

- The poem is a **dramatic monologue** in which we hear the voice of a Sikh man who works in his father's shop.

- He describes his daily routine, problems and dreams.

- The man is recently married to an unconventional Sikh wife. Both seem dissatisfied with life and spend their evenings dreaming together.

- Through his descriptions of others he reveals aspects of himself.

Ideas, Themes and Issues

- **Racism**: The customers are overly critical of the man, his shop and goods, and label his shop as 'Indian'.

- **Alienation and assimilation**: The Indian community is distinct from the rest of the neighbourhood. The wife's clothes and the things she does are a mix of two cultures.

- **Modern urban lives**: The precinct and shop are mundane and unromantic.

- **Clashing generations**: The man and his wife don't share the same values as his parents.

- **Sexual desire, passion and love**: The man often thinks about his wife and takes every opportunity to be with her. His desire for her and pleasure in their relationship is clear.

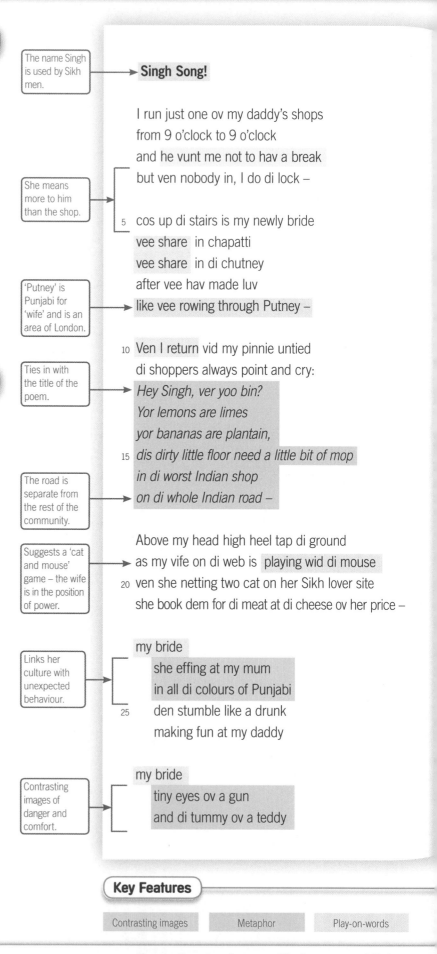

The name Singh is used by Sikh men.

Singh Song!

I run just one ov my daddy's shops
from 9 o'clock to 9 o'clock
and he vunt me not to hav a break

She means more to him than the shop.

but ven nobody in, I do di lock –

5 cos up di stairs is my newly bride
vee share in chapatti
vee share in di chutney
after vee hav made luv

'Putney' is Punjabi for 'wife' and is an area of London.

like vee rowing through Putney –

10 Ven I return vid my pinnie untied
di shoppers always point and cry:

Ties in with the title of the poem.

Hey Singh, ver yoo bin?
Yor lemons are limes
yor bananas are plantain,
15 *dis dirty little floor need a little bit of mop*
in di worst Indian shop

The road is separate from the rest of the community.

on di whole Indian road –

Above my head high heel tap di ground

Suggests a 'cat and mouse' game – the wife is in the position of power.

as my vife on di web is playing wid di mouse
20 ven she netting two cat on her Sikh lover site
she book dem for di meat at di cheese ov her price –

my bride

Links her culture with unexpected behaviour.

she effing at my mum
in all di colours of Punjabi
25 den stumble like a drunk
making fun at my daddy

my bride

Contrasting images of danger and comfort.

tiny eyes ov a gun
and di tummy ov a teddy

Key Features

| Contrasting images | Metaphor | Play-on-words |

Dramatic monologue • First person • Idiolect

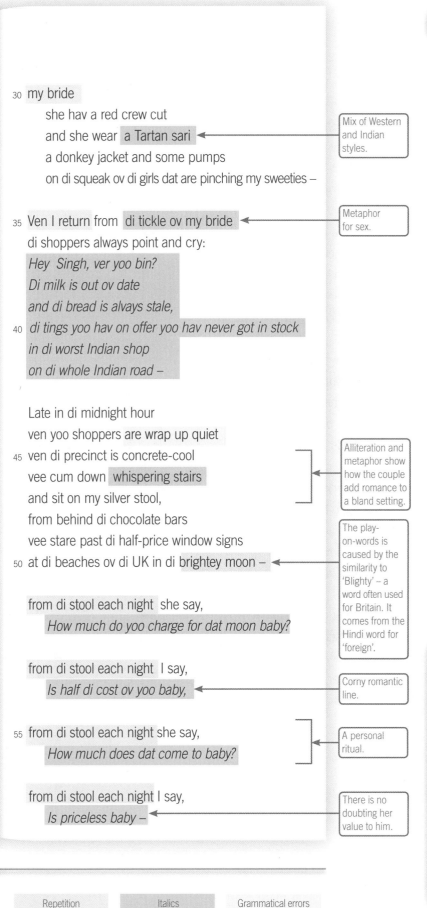

30 my bride

she hav a red crew cut

and she wear a Tartan sari ◄──── Mix of Western and Indian styles.

a donkey jacket and some pumps

on di squeak ov di girls dat are pinching my sweeties –

35 Ven I return from di tickle ov my bride ◄──── Metaphor for sex.

di shoppers always point and cry:

Hey Singh, ver yoo bin?

Di milk is out ov date

and di bread is alvays stale,

40 *di tings yoo hav on offer yoo hav never got in stock*

in di worst Indian shop

on di whole Indian road –

Late in di midnight hour

ven yoo shoppers are wrap up quiet

45 ven di precinct is concrete-cool

vee cum down whispering stairs ┐
│◄── Alliteration and metaphor show how the couple add romance to a bland setting.
and sit on my silver stool, ┘

from behind di chocolate bars

vee stare past di half-price window signs

50 at di beaches ov di UK in di brightey moon – ◄── The play-on-words is caused by the similarity to 'Blighty' – a word often used for Britain. It comes from the Hindi word for 'foreign'.

from di stool each night she say,

How much do yoo charge for dat moon baby?

from di stool each night I say,

Is half di cost ov yoo baby, ◄── Corny romantic line.

55 from di stool each night she say,

How much does dat come to baby? ◄── A personal ritual.

from di stool each night I say,

Is priceless baby – ◄── There is no doubting her value to him.

Repetition   Italics   Grammatical errors

Metaphor • Possessive pronoun

Form, Structure and Language

- The poem is written in the **first person**. This makes it feel very intimate.

- **Idiolect** creates a unique voice and shows that this is a personal story.

- **Contrasting images** and **metaphors** are used to suggest the unpredictable nature of the wife.

- The boisterous tone, rhymes and **play-on-words** reflect the personalities of the man and his wife.

- The wife is always in the man's thoughts. The **repetition** of the **possessive pronoun** 'my' shows his pride in her.

- **Grammatical errors** highlight that the voice in the poem is not a native English speaker.

- The use of **italics** for the customers' voices emphasises the regularity of their complaints and seems chorus-like.

Quick Test

1. How do we know that the wife is unpredictable?

2. What is the effect of the change in metre and rhyme of the final section?

3. Why do you think the poem is called 'Singh Song!'?

4. What is the effect of the repeated chorus of customers' voices?

Brendon Gallacher

Brendon Gallacher

He was seven and I was six, my Brendon Gallacher.
He was Irish and I was Scottish, my Brendon Gallacher.
His father was in prison; he was a cat burglar.
My father was a Communist Party full-time worker.
5 He had six brothers and I had one, my Brendon Gallacher.

He would hold my hand and take me by the river
where we'd talk all about his family being poor.
He'd get his mum out of Glasgow when he got older.
A wee holiday some place nice. Some place far.
10 I'd tell my mum about my Brendon Gallacher.

How his mum drank and his daddy was a cat burglar.
And she'd say, 'Why not have him round to dinner?'
No, no, I'd say, he's got big holes in his trousers.
I like meeting him by the burn in the open air.
15 Then one day after we'd been friends for two years,

one day when it was pouring and I was indoors,
my mum says to me, 'I was talking to Mrs Moir
who lives next door to your Brendon Gallacher.
Didn't you say his address was 24 Novar?
20 She says there are no Gallachers at 24 Novar.

There never have been any Gallachers next door.'
And he died then, my Brendon Gallacher,
flat out on my bedroom floor, his spiky hair,
his impish grin, his funny, flapping ear.
25 Oh Brendon. Oh my Brendon Gallacher.

Annotations (left side):

Use of the past tense shows this is a memory recalled.

Suggests she is making sense of her father's job.

Creates a realistic, personal tone.

Gives a story-like feel.

Lots of detail emphasises the significance of the event.

Reinforces the idea of loss/mourning and emphasises his 'realness' to her.

Wistful in tone.

Annotations (right side):

Shows her feelings of ownership of him.

She sees him outdoors, away from her family home.

Locates the incident in a specific place and suggests negative feelings about it.

Naive/childlike to think this detail would put her mother off.

Pathetic fallacy – the weather reflects the events that will follow. She is inside, a place where Brendon doesn't belong.

Separated from the rest of the direct speech increases the impact of the revelation.

Details of his appearance, bringing him to life.

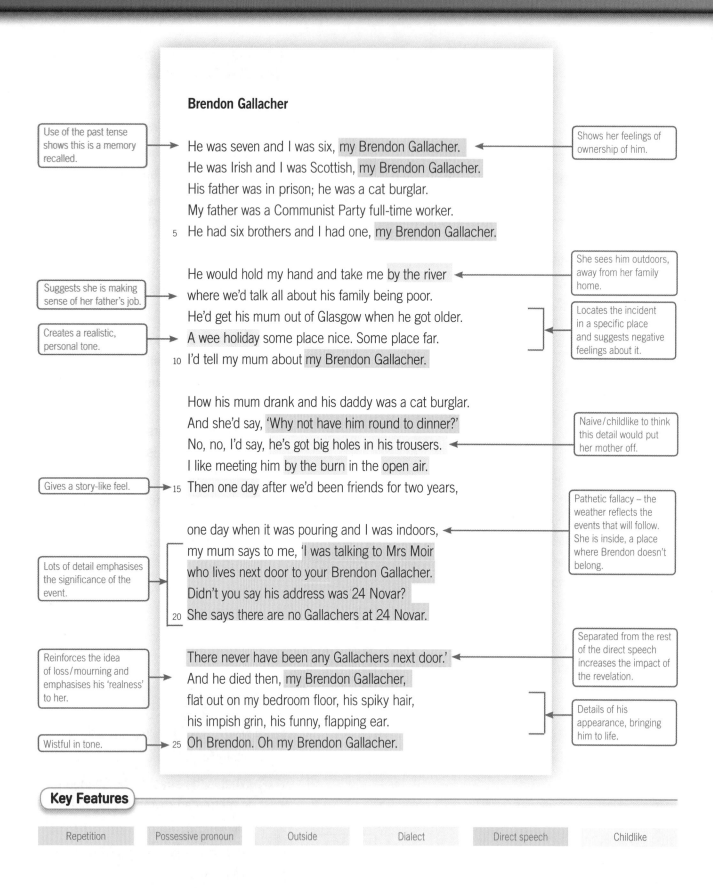

Key Features

| Repetition | Possessive pronoun | Outside | Dialect | Direct speech | Childlike |

First person • Autobiographical • Elegy • Stanza

Brendon Gallacher

About the Poem

- Written by **Jackie Kay** (1961–).
- The **first person** narrator recalls an imaginary friend from her childhood and describes the differences between his life and hers.
- She tries to keep him separate from the rest of her life, but her mother doesn't understand this and encourages her to include him in her life.
- When it's revealed that Brendon is an imaginary friend, he dies and is lost to the girl forever.
- The poem has **autobiographical** elements as there are similarities with Kay's own childhood.

Ideas, Themes and Issues

- **Childhood:** Brendon represents the freedom that children crave and which is often absent from the adult world. The narrator's ideas about poverty show a childish innocence.
- **Mourning/loss:** The poem mourns the loss of childhood innocence and the friend.
- **Imagination:** The qualities and life that the narrator has given Brendon may reveal her naive desires or might represent the lives she imagines for the families her father works to protect. The mother's need for facts and her inability to embrace imagination destroys Brendon.

Form, Structure and Language

- The poem is an **elegy**. Elegies are associated with mourning, showing us how important and real the loss of Brendon was.
- The **first three stanzas** begin with a focus on Brendon, emphasising his importance to her.
- **Repetition** and the **possessive pronouns** used by the narrator and her mother emphasise her feelings of ownership.
- **Direct speech** highlights the contrast between the adult's and child's view of the world.
- The use of **dialect** makes the poem feel very personal.
- The **childish language** and **half rhyme** create a wistful tone and impression of a memory recalled from childhood. The narrator looks back at both Brendon and her younger self with sad fondness.
- The grief at Brendon's loss is shown through **pathetic fallacy** and is made clear in the last line of the poem.

Quick Test

1. What are elegies usually associated with?
2. Why might the girl have created Brendon?
3. What is the significance of the weather the day Brendon dies?
4. Why might the mother want to know more about Brendon?

Give

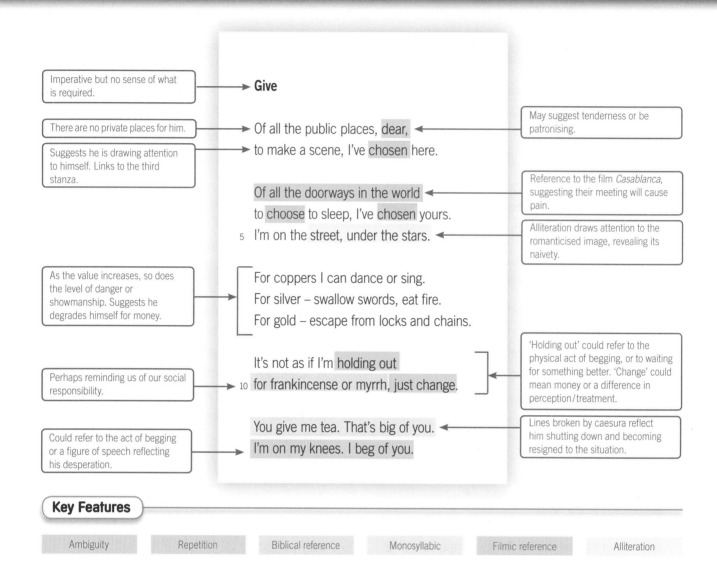

Imperative but no sense of what is required.

There are no private places for him.

Suggests he is drawing attention to himself. Links to the third stanza.

May suggest tenderness or be patronising.

Reference to the film *Casablanca*, suggesting their meeting will cause pain.

Alliteration draws attention to the romanticised image, revealing its naivety.

As the value increases, so does the level of danger or showmanship. Suggests he degrades himself for money.

Perhaps reminding us of our social responsibility.

'Holding out' could refer to the physical act of begging, or to waiting for something better. 'Change' could mean money or a difference in perception/treatment.

Could refer to the act of begging or a figure of speech reflecting his desperation.

Lines broken by caesura reflect him shutting down and becoming resigned to the situation.

Give

Of all the public places, dear,
to make a scene, I've chosen here.

Of all the doorways in the world
to choose to sleep, I've chosen yours.
5 I'm on the street, under the stars.

For coppers I can dance or sing.
For silver – swallow swords, eat fire.
For gold – escape from locks and chains.

It's not as if I'm holding out
10 for frankincense or myrrh, just change.

You give me tea. That's big of you.
I'm on my knees. I beg of you.

Key Features

| Ambiguity | Repetition | Biblical reference | Monosyllabic | Filmic reference | Alliteration |

About the Poem

- Written by **Simon Armitage** (1963–).

- The poem is narrated through the voice of a homeless person who is sleeping in a doorway.

- The man challenges our perceptions by talking directly to us and describes the attention-grabbing stunts he performs for change.

- He doesn't appreciate the token gestures that he is offered and wants something more.

Ideas, Themes and Issues

- **Social responsibility**: We have a responsibility to help vulnerable people but we need to listen to what they want rather than making assumptions or token gestures.

- **Homelessness**: Our assumptions about homelessness are presented and challenged. The character in the poem wants to be seen and heard more than he wants money.

Form, Structure and Language

- The poem is written in the **first person** and **present tense** which makes it very personal and immediate. It's very hard for both the reader and the person the man addresses in the poem to ignore this direct approach.

- The **opening** of the poem is **ambiguous**. We may think an adult is talking to a child, or that a couple is arguing. How we interpret those lines influences the way we see the relationship between the characters: tender or patronising.

- The **regularity of the syllable** count of each line suggests the man's restraint and control.

- As the man becomes despondent and resigned to the situation, he becomes **monosyllabic**.

- Repeated references to **choices** challenge the belief that homeless people have a choice about the way they live.

- **Alliteration** draws our attention to a romantic image that seems out of place.

- The **biblical** reference to the wise men in line 10 reminds us of our social responsibility.

- A **filmic reference** and **colloquialisms** create a light tone but as the poem progresses, it becomes more pleading and desperate.

Quick Test

1. Why have the words 'chosen' / 'choose' been repeated in the first two stanzas?

2. How does the language suggest that our attempts to help are sometimes patronising?

3. Which line has a romantic image, and why might it have been used?

4. The final line of the poem is ambiguous in its meaning. How could it be interpreted?

Monosyllabic • Alliteration • Biblical • Colloquialism

Les Grands Seigneurs

French for 'The Great Lords', romanticising them and giving them an air of chivalry.

Suggests the different roles that men fulfilled and her naivety.

Metaphors suggest a lack of dignity.

Caesura emphasises these ideas and her pride. Desired but unobtainable.

Internal rhyme highlights the lack of delay between the two.

Suggests a question posed by someone listening/reading this and refers to the wedding night.

Les Grands Seigneurs

Men were my buttresses, my castellated towers,
the bowers where I took my rest. The best and worst
of times were men: the peacocks and the cockatoos,
the nightingales, the strutting pink flamingos.

5 Men were my dolphins, my performing seals; my sailing-ships,
the ballast in my hold. They were the rocking-horses
prancing down the promenade, the bandstand
where the music played. My hurdy-gurdy monkey-men.

I was their queen. I sat enthroned before them,
10 out of reach. We played at courtly love:
the troubadour, the damsel and the peach.

But after I was wedded, bedded, I became
(yes, overnight) a toy, a plaything, little woman,
wife, a bit of fluff. My husband clicked
15 his fingers, called my bluff.

Metaphors suggest vain men who actively pursued her.

Nautical imagery.

'Played' suggests a childish innocence and emphasises this isn't reality. (Courtly love refers to the conventions guiding an affair between the upper classes.)

Suggests youth and beauty and perhaps virginity.

The listing of nouns links to the way she described men previously.

Commanding/controlling her.

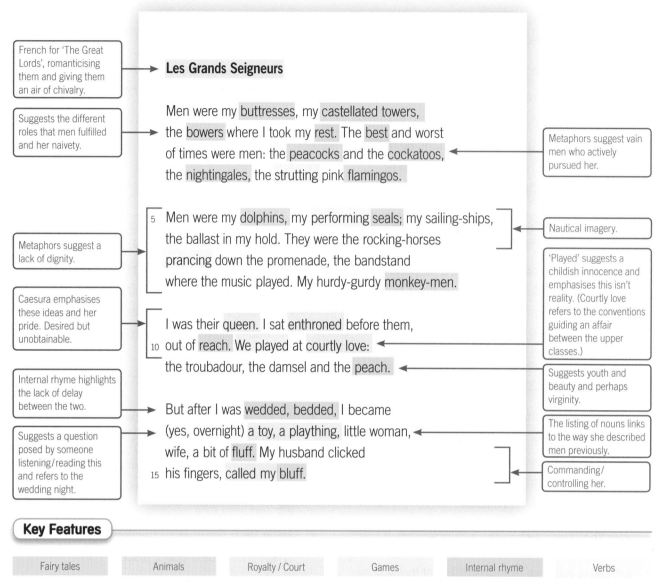

Key Features

| Fairy tales | Animals | Royalty / Court | Games | Internal rhyme | Verbs |

Naive • Metaphor

About the Poem

- Written by **Dorothy Molloy** (1942–2004).

- The voice in the poem belongs to a woman who describes her relationships with 'the great lords' of her past.

- She had been worshipped by men who tried to impress her. She saw these men both as fun diversions and as a way of protecting herself.

- Now she is married, the power has shifted and her husband has the upper hand.

Ideas, Themes and Issues

- **Power**: The woman was once pursued by men who tried to please her. She felt she was in control and they gave her both pleasure and protection. When she married, she lost this power.

- **Love and marriage**: Marriage has revealed the naivety of her expectations and how romanticised her view of marriage was. She has been reduced to being her husband's plaything.

- **Women and men**: Although the language in this poem is unique, the experiences of this character could describe the way in which women are often treated in relationships with men.

Form, Structure and Language

- The numerous references to games, diversions, castles and fairy tales show us how **naive** the woman was.

- The **French title**, a language often associated with love, might suggest that her memories of her lovers are overly **romanticised**.

- **Metaphors** and **hyperbole** are used to describe the men and make them seem undignified. There are lots of metaphors linking the men to birds, all of which actively pursue their mate.

- The **longer lines** in the first two **stanzas** indicate how cherished her memories are.

- The final stanza describes the present and the **shorter line length** reveals her frustration, disappointment and how she feels diminished.

- The **techniques** used earlier in the poem are turned on their heads in the final stanza. She finds herself her husband's plaything and is described through a list, which is how she described her men earlier in the poem.

Quick Test

1. What do the references to games, diversions, castles and fairy tales suggest?

2. What is the effect of the references to games and toys in the last stanza?

3. How does the structure of the poem reflect its meaning?

4. Were all her experiences of men positive before she was married?

Hyperbole • Stanza

Ozymandias

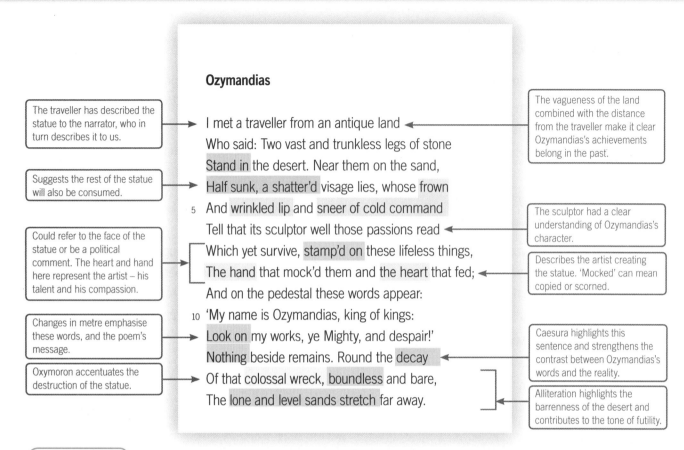

Ozymandias

The traveller has described the statue to the narrator, who in turn describes it to us.

> I met a traveller from an antique land
> Who said: Two vast and trunkless legs of stone
> Stand in the desert. Near them on the sand,
> Half sunk, a shatter'd visage lies, whose frown
> 5 And wrinkled lip and sneer of cold command
> Tell that its sculptor well those passions read
> Which yet survive, stamp'd on these lifeless things,
> The hand that mock'd them and the heart that fed;
> And on the pedestal these words appear:
> 10 'My name is Ozymandias, king of kings:
> Look on my works, ye Mighty, and despair!'
> Nothing beside remains. Round the decay
> Of that colossal wreck, boundless and bare,
> The lone and level sands stretch far away.

Suggests the rest of the statue will also be consumed.

Could refer to the face of the statue or be a political comment. The heart and hand here represent the artist – his talent and his compassion.

Changes in metre emphasise these words, and the poem's message.

Oxymoron accentuates the destruction of the statue.

The vagueness of the land combined with the distance from the traveller make it clear Ozymandias's achievements belong in the past.

The sculptor had a clear understanding of Ozymandias's character.

Describes the artist creating the statue. 'Mocked' can mean copied or scorned.

Caesura highlights this sentence and strengthens the contrast between Ozymandias's words and the reality.

Alliteration highlights the barrenness of the desert and contributes to the tone of futility.

Key Features

| Change in metre | Alliteration | Ozymandias's character | Synecdoche | Destruction/Decay | Oxymoron |

About the Poem

- Written by **Percy Bysshe Shelley** (1792–1822).

- The narrator of the poem recounts an anonymous traveller's tale.

- The narrator re-tells the traveller's description of the remains of a vast, ruined statue of Ozymandias, the ancient Egyptian Pharaoh Rameses II.

- The statue is a **metaphor** and reveals the Pharaoh's character and the foolishness of his pride.

- In effect, the poem focuses on two voices – those of the traveller and Ozymandias, and two characters – the artist and Ozymandias.

- The poem can be seen as an analogy: time will challenge any great civilisation or ruler.

Ideas, Themes and Issues

- **Death and mortality**: The desert symbolises the passing of time that erases all traces of Ozymandias and reminds us that death comes to us all.

- **Power**: Ozymandias's power was absolute. The face of the statue and the words on the pedestal reveal his character. We feel no sympathy for him.

- **Pride**: The vast size of the statue reflects Ozymandias's pride. The **futility** of his pride is demonstrated by the ruin of the statue and his achievements. His name is significant as it is derived from the Greek, 'ozium' (air) and 'mandate' (rule) and means he is 'ruler of nothing'.

- **Art**: The achievements of the sculptor outlive those of Ozymandias.

Form, Structure and Language

- The poem is a **sonnet** written in **iambic pentameter**. Traditionally sonnets are associated with love poetry, but here political ideas are explored.

- The poem can be divided into **three parts**. The words of the traveller create a picture of Ozymandias in the first and last part. The middle part introduces the idea of art enduring using **synecdoche** to represent the artist.

- The use of **oxymoron** highlights the destruction of the statue.

- The broken statue **symbolises** that power and achievements are weakened by time. The **irony** is that the artist's work remains.

- Ozymandias's words would have inspired **awe and fear**, but now they cause **despair** as they are evidence that even the power of the mighty is temporary.

- Ozymandias's self-given title, 'king of kings', reveals his pride and contrasts with the literal translation of his name.

Quick Test

1. How do the setting and narrator contribute to our sense of Ozymandias's diminished power?

2. What does the poem suggest about the nature of power?

3. How does the poet create a negative impression of Ozymandias's character?

4. What is the effect of the last two lines of the poem?

My Last Duchess

About the Poem

- Written by **Robert Browning** (1812–1889).

- In this poem we hear the voice of a Duke describing a portrait of his late wife to a visiting servant, who is helping arrange a marriage between the Duke and his master's daughter.

- The Duke unwittingly reveals the true character of both himself and the Duchess through the things he says.

- We learn that the Duke had his wife killed as he suspected she was unfaithful to him.

- The Duke boasts about the beautiful objects he owns, unaware of the effect of his words.

Ideas, Themes and Issues

- **Violence:** The Duke's lack of remorse at having his wife murdered is shocking.

- **Power and control:** The Duke is obsessed with maintaining his power over his wife. He is so powerful that she is killed at his request.

- **Jealousy:** The Duke is jealous of the attention that his wife gives to others and wants to be the only person in her favour.

- **Pride:** The Duke is proud of his name and feels the Duchess doesn't respect its value. The manner in which he describes his possessions also reveals his pride. Ultimately, it is his pride which leads him to have his wife killed.

My Last Duchess

Ferrara

That's my last Duchess painted on the wall,
Looking as if she were alive. I call
That piece a wonder, now: Frà Pandolf's hands
Worked busily a day, and there she stands.
5 Will't please you sit and look at her? I said
'Frà Pandolf' by design, for never read
Strangers like you that pictured countenance,
The depth and passion of its earnest glance,
But to myself they turned (since none puts by
10 The curtain I have drawn for you, but I)
And seemed as they would ask me, if they durst,
How such a glance came there; so, not the first
Are you to turn and ask thus. Sir, 'twas not
Her husband's presence only, called that spot
15 Of joy into the Duchess' cheek: perhaps
Frà Pandolf chanced to say 'Her mantle laps
Over my lady's wrist too much,' or 'Paint
Must never hope to reproduce the faint
Half-flush that dies along her throat': such stuff
20 Was courtesy, she thought, and cause enough
For calling up that spot of joy. She had
A heart – how shall I say? – too soon made glad,
Too easily impressed; she liked whate'er
She looked on, and her looks went everywhere.
25 Sir, 'twas all one! My favour at her breast,
The dropping of the daylight in the West,
The bough of cherries some officious fool
Broke in the orchard for her, the white mule

Annotations:

- Positive description. Compare with lines 13–34. → (points to line 8)

- A positive image, framed in a negative light by his perceptions. → (points to lines 14–15)

- Self-interruptions suggest spontaneity, although it is a rehearsed speech. → (points to line 22)

- Implies she was unfaithful, or at least, looked at other men. → (points to lines 23–24)

Key Features

Duchess's qualities   Possessive pronouns   Self interruption

Dramatic monologue • First person • Possessive pronoun

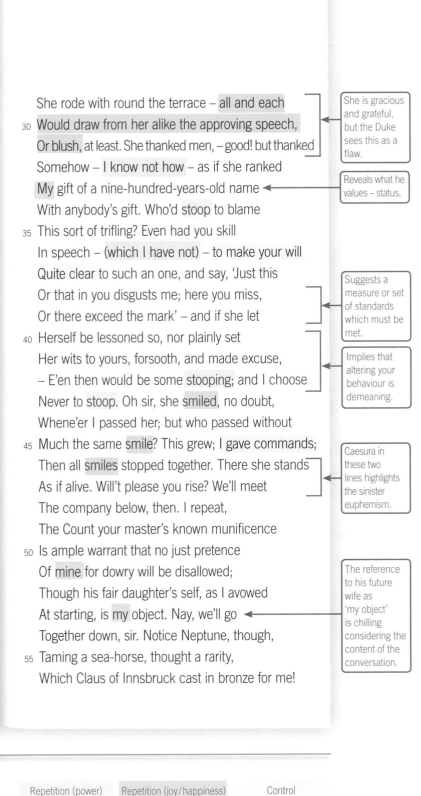

She rode with round the terrace – all and each
30 Would draw from her alike the approving speech,
Or blush, at least. She thanked men, – good! but thanked
Somehow – I know not how – as if she ranked
My gift of a nine-hundred-years-old name
With anybody's gift. Who'd stoop to blame
35 This sort of trifling? Even had you skill
In speech – (which I have not) – to make your will
Quite clear to such an one, and say, 'Just this
Or that in you disgusts me; here you miss,
Or there exceed the mark' – and if she let
40 Herself be lessoned so, nor plainly set
Her wits to yours, forsooth, and made excuse,
– E'en then would be some stooping; and I choose
Never to stoop. Oh sir, she smiled, no doubt,
Whene'er I passed her; but who passed without
45 Much the same smile? This grew; I gave commands;
Then all smiles stopped together. There she stands
As if alive. Will't please you rise? We'll meet
The company below, then. I repeat,
The Count your master's known munificence
50 Is ample warrant that no just pretence
Of mine for dowry will be disallowed;
Though his fair daughter's self, as I avowed
At starting, is my object. Nay, we'll go
Together down, sir. Notice Neptune, though,
55 Taming a sea-horse, thought a rarity,
Which Claus of Innsbruck cast in bronze for me!

Annotations:
- She is gracious and grateful, but the Duke sees this as a flaw.
- Reveals what he values – status.
- Suggests a measure or set of standards which must be met.
- Implies that altering your behaviour is demeaning.
- Caesura in these two lines highlights the sinister euphemism.
- The reference to his future wife as 'my object' is chilling considering the content of the conversation.

Repetition (power)   Repetition (joy/happiness)   Control

Form, Structure and Language

- The poem is a **dramatic monologue** which is presented as a conversation. The **first person** narrative allows us to fully understand the Duke's actions and motivations, perhaps even where he doesn't recognise them himself.

- His **descriptions of his wife** reveal a kind woman, which make us sympathetic towards her and show the depth of the Duke's need to control her.

- **Repetition** suggests the Duke's preoccupation with certain ideas and behaviours.

- The continued use of **possessive pronouns** reflects the Duke's selfish and proud personality.

- The poem is organised into **rhyming couplets** but because the lines are not **end-stopped** the rhyme isn't obvious. This pushes the poem on, as the Duke relentlessly pursues his next marriage.

Quick Test

1. How does the poem's structure reflect the Duke's present concerns?

2. Why do we learn about the Duke's actions from his own mouth?

3. What is the effect of the repetition in lines 34–43 and 43–46?

4. Why does the poem end with the Duke describing another piece of art?

Rhyming couplet • End-stopped

The River God

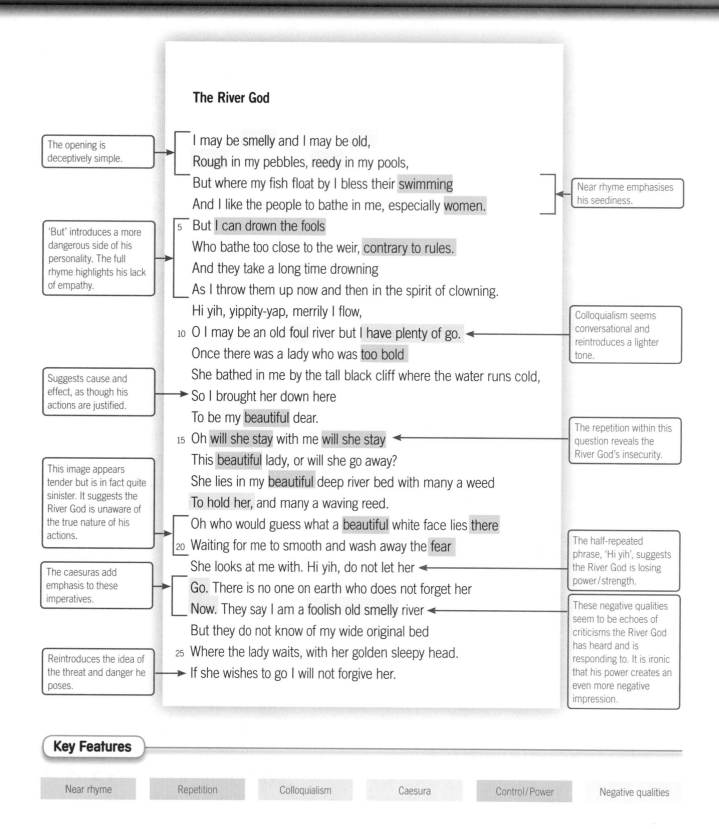

The River God

The opening is deceptively simple.

I may be smelly and I may be old,
Rough in my pebbles, reedy in my pools,
But where my fish float by I bless their swimming
And I like the people to bathe in me, especially women.

Near rhyme emphasises his seediness.

'But' introduces a more dangerous side of his personality. The full rhyme highlights his lack of empathy.

5 But I can drown the fools
Who bathe too close to the weir, contrary to rules.
And they take a long time drowning
As I throw them up now and then in the spirit of clowning.
Hi yih, yippity-yap, merrily I flow,
10 O I may be an old foul river but I have plenty of go.

Colloquialism seems conversational and reintroduces a lighter tone.

Suggests cause and effect, as though his actions are justified.

Once there was a lady who was too bold
She bathed in me by the tall black cliff where the water runs cold,
So I brought her down here
To be my beautiful dear.

15 Oh will she stay with me will she stay

The repetition within this question reveals the River God's insecurity.

This image appears tender but is in fact quite sinister. It suggests the River God is unaware of the true nature of his actions.

This beautiful lady, or will she go away?
She lies in my beautiful deep river bed with many a weed
To hold her, and many a waving reed.
Oh who would guess what a beautiful white face lies there
20 Waiting for me to smooth and wash away the fear
She looks at me with. Hi yih, do not let her

The half-repeated phrase, 'Hi yih', suggests the River God is losing power/strength.

The caesuras add emphasis to these imperatives.

Go. There is no one on earth who does not forget her
Now. They say I am a foolish old smelly river
But they do not know of my wide original bed

These negative qualities seem to be echoes of criticisms the River God has heard and is responding to. It is ironic that his power creates an even more negative impression.

Reintroduces the idea of the threat and danger he poses.

25 Where the lady waits, with her golden sleepy head.
If she wishes to go I will not forgive her.

Key Features

| Near rhyme | Repetition | Colloquialism | Caesura | Control/Power | Negative qualities |

Personification • Dramatic monologue • Free verse • First person

About the Poem

- Written by **Stevie Smith** (1902–1971).

- The river is **personified** and is given the persona of the River God. It is this voice that we hear in the poem.

- The River God seems to be old, smelly and helpless but as the poem progresses a seedy, dark and dangerous side is revealed.

- He has a weakness for women and takes one for a companion, but his insecurity makes him question whether he will be able to keep her.

Ideas, Themes and Issues

- **Power**: Like the gods in Greek mythology, the River God is powerful but also petty, jealous and vengeful. He meddles in human lives with no thought for the consequences.

- **Isolation**: The River God is lonely. His only companion has been taken by force and he knows that he has a tenuous hold on her.

- **Revenge**: He punishes those who don't play by his rules and threatens to take revenge on his companion if she leaves him.

Form, Structure and Language

- The poem is a **dramatic monologue** written in **free verse**. The **first person** account reveals more about the River God than he intends.

- At first the **tone** of the poem appears light-hearted but it becomes **sinister** and **macabre**.

- The mix of **enjambment**, **end-stopped** lines and the **varied rhythm and rhyme** mimic the ever-changing currents and moods of the river and his unpredictable character.

- **Repetition** of the word 'beautiful' shows his fascination with the woman and his fixation on her appearance.

- The **rhyming couplets** create a jaunty air, but this doesn't disguise the dark tone that's created by the pleasure the River God takes in tormenting people.

- The description of people as 'fools', and the **rhyme** linking 'clowning' and 'drowning' show the River God's lack of **empathy**.

Quick Test

1. How would you describe the tone of the first two lines?

2. Why might Smith have chosen a god to represent the spirit of the river?

3. In which line does the River God use a gentle image to hide the truth about what has happened to the woman he has taken?

4. What is the effect of the last line of the poem?

The Hunchback in the Park

About the Poem

- Written by **Dylan Thomas** (1914–1953).

- The voice in the poem belongs to a young boy (possibly based on Thomas himself) who describes what he sees in his local park.

- A lonely hunchback visits each day and is taunted by a group of boys who have also escaped to the park.

- The park symbolises freedom for the boys and for the hunchback. Inside it, their imaginations run free.

Ideas, Themes and Issues

- **Isolation**: The hunchback is isolated because of his appearance. The young narrator is also isolated as he is clearly not a part of the group of truant boys.

- **Imagination**: All of the characters use their imaginations to fill in what is missing from their lives. The park seems only to exist when the young boy is there; it is a place of the imagination.

- **The artist**: The hunchback is a **metaphor** for poets (and could be based on Thomas as an adult) and an example of **synecdoche**. Poets and artistic people are often misunderstood but they create beautiful things from their imaginations.

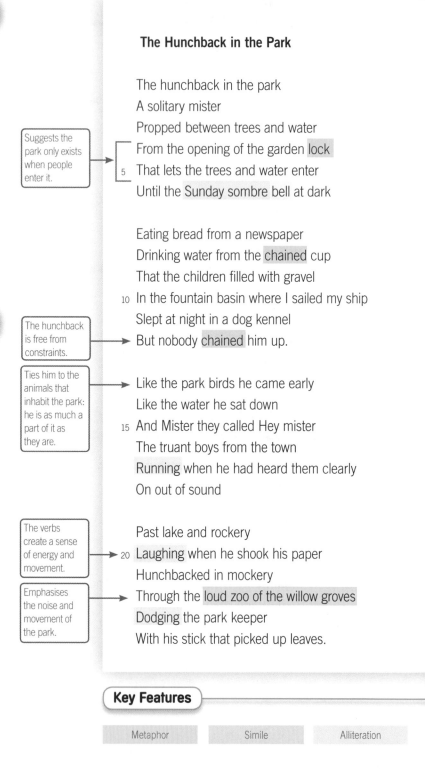

The Hunchback in the Park

The hunchback in the park
A solitary mister
Propped between trees and water
From the opening of the garden lock
5 That lets the trees and water enter
Until the Sunday sombre bell at dark

Eating bread from a newspaper
Drinking water from the chained cup
That the children filled with gravel
10 In the fountain basin where I sailed my ship
Slept at night in a dog kennel
But nobody chained him up.

Like the park birds he came early
Like the water he sat down
15 And Mister they called Hey mister
The truant boys from the town
Running when he had heard them clearly
On out of sound

Past lake and rockery
20 Laughing when he shook his paper
Hunchbacked in mockery
Through the loud zoo of the willow groves
Dodging the park keeper
With his stick that picked up leaves.

Suggests the park only exists when people enter it.

The hunchback is free from constraints.

Ties him to the animals that inhabit the park: he is as much a part of it as they are.

The verbs create a sense of energy and movement.

Emphasises the noise and movement of the park.

Key Features

| Metaphor | Simile | Alliteration |

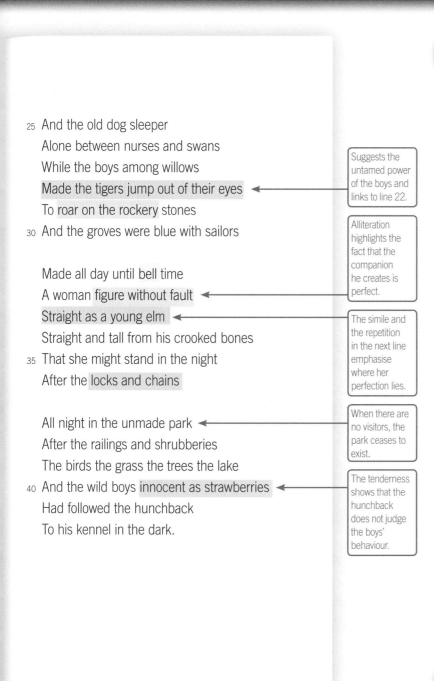

25 And the old dog sleeper
Alone between nurses and swans
While the boys among willows
Made the tigers jump out of their eyes
To roar on the rockery stones
30 And the groves were blue with sailors

Made all day until bell time
A woman figure without fault
Straight as a young elm
Straight and tall from his crooked bones
35 That she might stand in the night
After the locks and chains

All night in the unmade park
After the railings and shrubberies
The birds the grass the trees the lake
40 And the wild boys innocent as strawberries
Had followed the hunchback
To his kennel in the dark.

Suggests the untamed power of the boys and links to line 22.

Alliteration highlights the fact that the companion he creates is perfect.

The simile and the repetition in the next line emphasise where her perfection lies.

When there are no visitors, the park ceases to exist.

The tenderness shows that the hunchback does not judge the boys' behaviour.

Verbs   Locks and chains   Bells

Form, Structure and Language

- There are many **examples of contrast** within the poem. The references to locks and chains contrast with the freedom that all the characters experience in the park. The hunchback creates a companion who is his opposite in appearance.

- The **lack of full stops** reflects the lack of restriction in imagination and is a continuation of the idea that the hunchback is free from **constraint**.

- **Imagery** is used to compare the boys and the hunchback to **animals**. The boys are presented as tigers, powerful and unrestrained, but the hunchback is a tame, obedient dog. This might suggest that the boys are the more free of the two.

- The **sound of bells** signalling the end of the day and the end of the park's existence, and the loneliness of both the young boy and the hunchback, create a **melancholic** tone.

Quick Test

1. What details in the poem suggest the hunchback isn't as pitiful as he might appear?

2. What is the effect of the narrator's descriptions of the group of boys?

3. Why is the companion that the hunchback creates important in this poem?

The Ruined Maid

The Ruined Maid

This familiar address suggests a close relationship between the people speaking.

Immediately, the friend comments on 'Melia's positively changed appearance.

The question implies her fate is common knowledge.

The details of poverty and labour are emphasised by alliteration.

This makes the link between her appearance and situation clear.

A further mention of 'Melia's appearance prompts the repetition of the way it was achieved.

An ironic statement.

The simile and alliteration combine to create a vivid picture of 'Melia's previous appearance.

Alliteration here draws attention to all the problems and hardships of 'Melia's former situation.

The friend is fixated on the details of 'Melia's changed appearance and either does not hear or care how this was managed.

Suggests arrogance on 'Melia's part and jealousy on the friend's.

The caesura here suggests an abrupt tone and highlights the contrast with what follows.

'Melia's composure slips and her roots are revealed or could this be her rebellion against conforming?

'O 'Melia, my dear, this does everything crown!
Who could have supposed I should meet you in Town?
And whence such fair garments, such prosperi-ty?' –
'O didn't you know I'd been ruined?' said she.

5 – 'You left us in tatters, without shoes or socks,
Tired of digging potatoes, and spudding up docks;
And now you've gay bracelets and bright feathers three!' –
'Yes: that's how we dress when we're ruined,' said she.

– 'At home in the barton you said "thee" and "thou",
10 And "thik oon", and "theas oon", and "t'other"; but now
Your talking quite fits 'ee for high compa-ny!' –
'Some polish is gained with one's ruin,' said she.

– 'Your hands were like paws then, your face blue and bleak
But now I'm bewitched by your delicate cheek,
15 And your little gloves fit as on any la-dy!' –
'We never do work when we're ruined,' said she.

– 'You used to call home-life a hag-ridden dream,
And you'd sigh, and you'd sock; but at present you seem
To know not of megrims or melancho-ly!' –
20 'True. One's pretty lively when ruined,' said she.

– 'I wish I had feathers, a fine sweeping gown,
And a delicate face, and could strut about Town!' –
'My dear – a raw country girl, such as you be,
Cannot quite expect that. You ain't ruined,' said she.

Key Features

| Repetition | Dialect | Alliteration | Simile | First person plural | Indefinite pronoun |

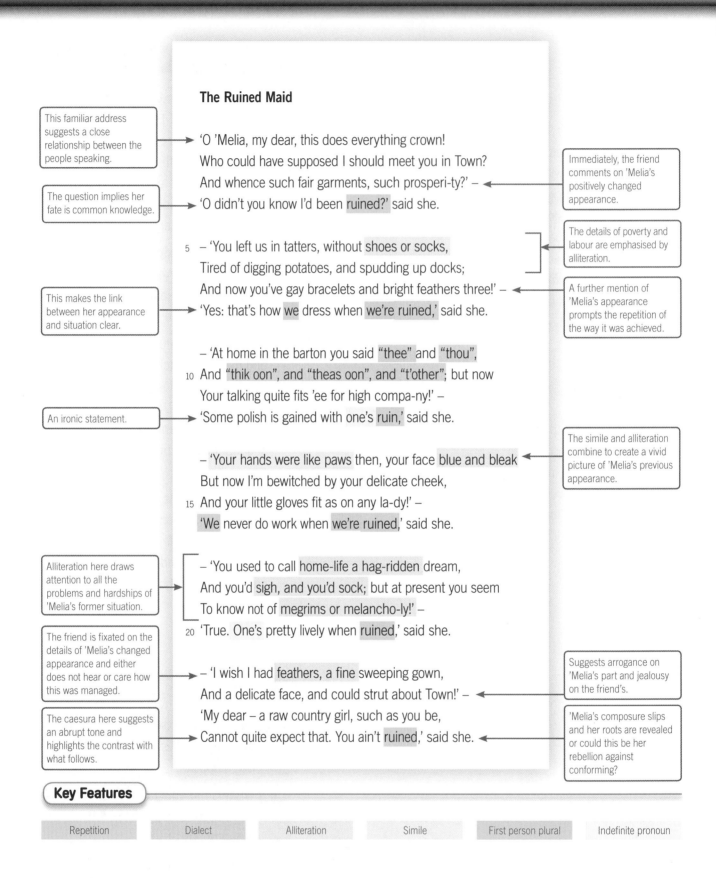

Dramatic duologue • Satirical • Rhyming couplet

About the Poem

- Written by **Thomas Hardy** (1840–1928).

- There are two female voices in the poem, belonging to friends who meet unexpectedly.

- One describes the changes in her friend's appearance and speech. We learn that the changes are a result of her turning to prostitution and this has 'ruined' her and made her unfit for marriage.

- The words from the ruined maid's mouth convey her attitude and hint that the changes came at a cost, despite her improved appearance.

Ideas, Themes and Issues

- **Morality**: Prostitution was one of the few ways that young women of low social status could improve their fortunes but the word 'ruin' itself is a negative judgement on them.

- **Appearances**: While her appearance has changed for the better, 'Melia is ruined while her friend who has the plainer appearance still has her reputation.

Form, Structure and Language

- The poem is a **dramatic duologue** between two young women. While the majority of what we hear is the voice of the unnamed friend, it is the character of 'Melia that we focus on.

- The **lack of 'Melia's voice** and the use of the **indefinite pronoun**, suggest her haughtiness.

- Repeated references to 'Melia's appearance could reflect the idea that people's perceptions of us are often based on superficial elements that do not represent the truth of a situation.

- The **repetition** of the word 'ruined' in 'Melia's lines reminds us of the cost of her transformation.

- A **satirical** tone is created by the **rhyming couplets** and 'Melia's repeated comments about ruination.

- The **dialect** and **colloquialisms** of the friend contrast with 'Melia's formal **Standard English**. Her 'true self' is shown by her language in the last **stanza**.

Quick Test

1. Is the poem as frivolous as it first seems?

2. Why might 'Melia have used the first person plural pronoun in the second stanza?

3. What is the effect of the final line of the poem?

4. Which details from the poem might suggest 'Melia feels superior to her friend?

Dialect • Colloquialism • Standard English • Stanza

Casehistory: Alison (head injury)

About the Poem

- Written by **U. A. Fanthorpe** (1929–2009).

- In this **dramatic monologue**, we hear the voice of Alison, a woman who has suffered a head injury.

- Alison looks at a photograph of herself when she was young and describes the girl in it as if she were a stranger.

- Alison remembers nothing of her past and even has to be reminded daily that her father is dead.

Ideas, Themes and Issues

- **Youth and age**: Alison looks back on a time of innocence. The girl in the photograph looks happy and her future is full of promise.

- **Mourning and loss**: Alison mourns for the person she once was and the promise her future held. She is also in a constant state of mourning for her father.

- **Personal identity**: We define ourselves through our memories and our relationships with the people around us. Alison has lost both of these things and can only create a sense of herself by comparing her present life to the details of her past that she gets from her photo.

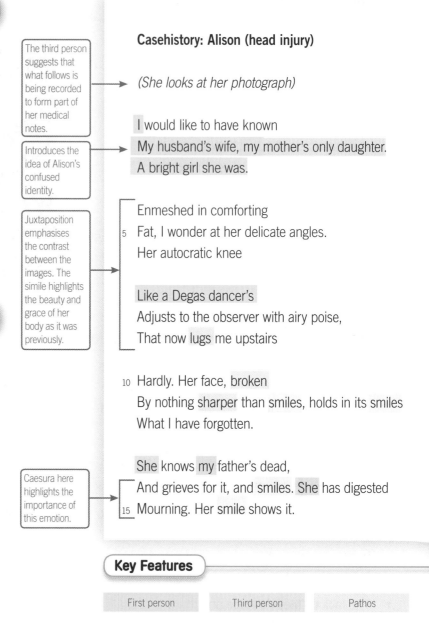

The third person suggests that what follows is being recorded to form part of her medical notes.

Introduces the idea of Alison's confused identity.

Juxtaposition emphasises the contrast between the images. The simile highlights the beauty and grace of her body as it was previously.

Caesura here highlights the importance of this emotion.

Casehistory: Alison (head injury)

(She looks at her photograph)

I would like to have known
My husband's wife, my mother's only daughter.
A bright girl she was.

Enmeshed in comforting
5 Fat, I wonder at her delicate angles.
Her autocratic knee

Like a Degas dancer's
Adjusts to the observer with airy poise,
That now lugs me upstairs

10 Hardly. Her face, broken
By nothing sharper than smiles, holds in its smiles
What I have forgotten.

She knows my father's dead,
And grieves for it, and smiles. She has digested
15 Mourning. Her smile shows it.

Key Features

| First person | Third person | Pathos |

Dramatic monologue • Stanza • First person

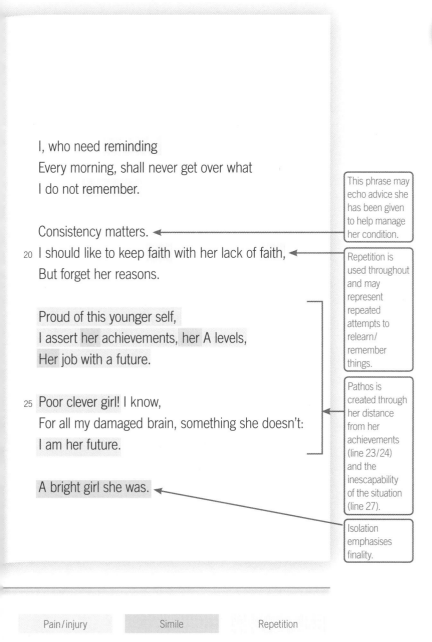

I, who need reminding
Every morning, shall never get over what
I do not remember.

Consistency matters. ◄

This phrase may echo advice she has been given to help manage her condition.

20 I should like to keep faith with her lack of faith, ◄
But forget her reasons.

Repetition is used throughout and may represent repeated attempts to relearn/ remember things.

Proud of this younger self,
I assert her achievements, her A levels,
Her job with a future.

25 Poor clever girl! I know,
For all my damaged brain, something she doesn't:
I am her future.

Pathos is created through her distance from her achievements (line 23/24) and the inescapability of the situation (line 27).

A bright girl she was. ◄

Isolation emphasises finality.

Pain/injury   Simile   Repetition

Form, Structure and Language

- The **regularity of the stanza length** and the **shortness** of the majority of the lines may reflect the repetitiveness of Alison's life and her need to break things down into manageable tasks.

- Use of both the **first person** and **third person** to describe herself highlights Alison's confusion.

- **Juxtaposed** images of her past and present life emphasise how much has changed for Alison and the difficulties of her present condition.

- The tone is **matter-of-fact** and lacks any self-pity, perhaps reflecting the tone of clinical notes suggested by the title.

- **Pathos** is created through Alison's admiration of her younger self and her understanding of what the future holds for the girl in the photograph.

- There are lots of references to **pain and injury** to remind us of Alison's accident and the lasting damage it has caused.

- Riddle-like statements in the first, sixth and seventh stanzas suggest Alison's confusion and her lack of a clear personal identity.

Quick Test

1. What do you think the purpose of the first italicised, bracketed line is?

2. What ideas about identity are presented in the poem?

3. What is the effect of the last line of the poem?

Third person • Juxtaposition • Pathos

On a Portrait of a Deaf Man

About the Poem

- Written by **John Betjeman** (1906–1984).

- The voice recalls memories of the poet's father, a deaf man.

- His father was a kind man who enjoyed simple pleasures.

- The voice can't separate the pleasant images of his father from images of his dead body and it is these images that he is left with.

Ideas, Themes and Issues

- **Mourning and loss**: The voice is haunted by images of his father's decaying body.

- **Memories**: He has affectionate memories of times he shared with his father and the things his father enjoyed.

- **Faith**: In the final **stanza**, he questions the existence of God as he can't accept the Christian message of life after death when he sees only physical decay.

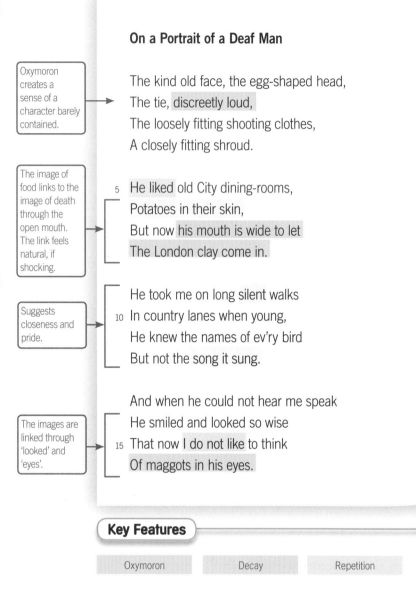

On a Portrait of a Deaf Man

Oxymoron creates a sense of a character barely contained.

The kind old face, the egg-shaped head,
The tie, discreetly loud,
The loosely fitting shooting clothes,
A closely fitting shroud.

The image of food links to the image of death through the open mouth. The link feels natural, if shocking.

5 He liked old City dining-rooms,
Potatoes in their skin,
But now his mouth is wide to let
The London clay come in.

Suggests closeness and pride.

He took me on long silent walks
10 In country lanes when young,
He knew the names of ev'ry bird
But not the song it sung.

The images are linked through 'looked' and 'eyes'.

And when he could not hear me speak
He smiled and looked so wise
15 That now I do not like to think
Of maggots in his eyes.

Key Features

Oxymoron   Decay   Repetition

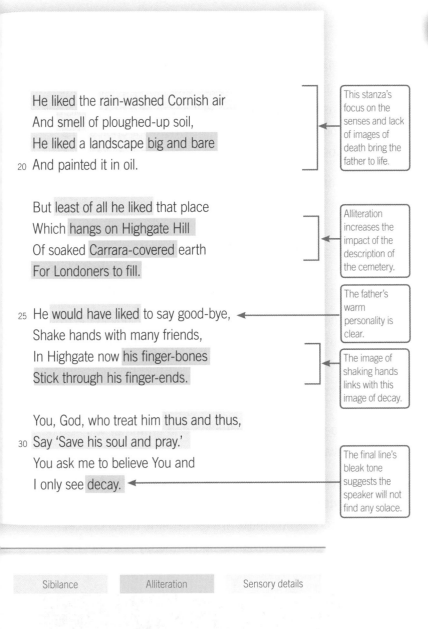

He liked the rain-washed Cornish air
And smell of ploughed-up soil,
He liked a landscape big and bare
20 And painted it in oil.

> This stanza's focus on the senses and lack of images of death bring the father to life.

But least of all he liked that place
Which hangs on Highgate Hill
Of soaked Carrara-covered earth
For Londoners to fill.

> Alliteration increases the impact of the description of the cemetery.

25 He would have liked to say good-bye,
Shake hands with many friends,
In Highgate now his finger-bones
Stick through his finger-ends.

> The father's warm personality is clear.

> The image of shaking hands links with this image of decay.

You, God, who treat him thus and thus,
30 Say 'Save his soul and pray.'
You ask me to believe You and
I only see decay.

> The final line's bleak tone suggests the speaker will not find any solace.

Sibilance   Alliteration   Sensory details

Form, Structure and Language

- The poem is an **elegy** written in **ballad** form. This mixture of forms may reflect his inability to separate **sentimental** memories of his father from his grief over his loss.

- The simple, **uncomplicated language** reflects the tastes of his father and doesn't soften the images of death and decay.

- The **juxtaposition** of past and present highlights the contrast between the father's enjoyment of life's simple pleasures and graphic images of decay.

- The tone is **nostalgic** where memories of the father are described and **matter-of-fact** where images of death and decay are presented.

- The father's kind, warm personality is revealed through affectionately recalled memories.

- The **images of decay** become increasingly **explicit**, adding to the horror we feel at the realities of death. This culminates in the **final stanza** where **sibilance** reveals his anger as he directly addresses God.

Quick Test

1. How does the first stanza prepare us for the stark contrasts in the stanzas that follow?

2. What details in the poem paint the picture of a kind man?

3. How is the final stanza different from the rest of the poem?

About The Exam

What to Expect

The exam is divided into two sections, Section A and Section B. **Section A focuses on the poetry from the *Moon on the Tides* anthology** and Section B focuses on unseen poetry.

The poems in the *Moon on the Tides* anthology are divided into four clusters:
- **Character and Voice**
- **Place**
- **Conflict**
- **Relationships**

Each cluster contains 15 poems. Some of these poems are from the **Literary Heritage** and some are **contemporary**, including poems from **different cultures**.

There will be a **choice of two questions** for each cluster. You must choose **one** of the questions to answer. The question will **name one poem** and ask you to **compare** it to a poem of your choice. The poem you choose must be from the **same cluster**.

Some poems will only be named on one tier:
- *Medusa, Les Grands Seigneurs* and *Casehistory: Alison (head injury)* will only be named on the higher tier paper.
- *Brendon Gallacher, Give* and *The Ruined Maid* will only be named on the foundation tier paper.

You will be given a copy of the anthology in the exam, but **it will not have any notes or annotations** on it.

What You Will Be Assessed On

In Section A you'll be assessed on how well you do the following:

AO1	Respond to texts critically and imaginatively, select and evaluate textual detail to illustrate and support interpretations.
AO2	Explain how **language**, **structure** and **form** contribute to writers' presentation of ideas, themes and settings.
AO3	Make **comparisons and explain links** between texts, evaluating writers' different ways of expressing meaning and achieving effects.

Your **spelling, punctuation and grammar** will also be awarded marks.

Remember that **you'll be awarded marks for the quality of your response** rather than for the number of points you make. It's far better to make **critical, insightful comments** than to merely point out the poet's techniques.

Allocating Your Time

You're advised to spend about 45 minutes on Section A. You could allocate your time as follows:
- **5–10 minutes** to **choose your question** and **make a plan**
- **30–35 minutes** to **write your answer**
- around **5 minutes** to **check your work** when you've finished.

Choosing Your Question

1 **Read both questions** for your cluster carefully.

2 **Highlight the key words** and think about how you would answer each question.

3 **Consider how much you know about the named poems and which poems** would offer the best comparison.

The table below suggests the main points of comparison between the poems in the cluster. It will help you identify poems to compare in the exam.

The crosses show the significant features of each poem so it's easy to see where the similarities and differences are.

		The Clown Punk	Checking Out Me History	Horse Whisperer	Medusa	Singh Song!	Brendon Gallacher	Give	Les Grands Seigneurs	Ozymandias	My Last Duchess	The River God	The Hunchback in the Park	The Ruined Maid	Casehistory: Alison (head injury)	On a Portrait of a Deaf Man
Themes / Key ideas	Youth	x				x	x						x			
	Mourning and loss			x			x		x						x	x
	Personal identity	x	x	x					x	x					x	
	Appearance	x											x	x		
	Outsiders / loneliness	x		x		x		x				x	x	x	x	
	Imagination						x						x			x
	Love, desire, jealousy				x	x			x		x	x				
	Power			x	x				x	x	x	x				
	State of mind				x			x							x	
Form / Structure	Sonnet	x								x						
	Dramatic monologue		x	x	x	x		x	x		x	x			x	x
	Elegy						x									x
	First person viewpoint		x	x	x	x	x	x	x		x	x			x	x
	Full rhyme		x							x	x	x			x	x
	Half rhyme	x			x	x							x	x		
Language	Imagery	x	x	x	x	x			x				x			
	Colloquialisms	x						x	x							
	Idiolect or dialect		x			x	x								x	
	Repetition		x	x	x	x	x	x			x	x			x	x
	Juxtaposition	x	x												x	x
	Sensory language			x												x
	Ambiguity				x			x		x					x	

Only the most obvious points of comparison are shown on this table. Use your knowledge of the poems to find unique features to create a personal response.

Planning Your Answer

How to Plan

Having a clear plan will help you to write a structured response and gives you something to refer back to if you get stuck while writing.

Your plan should be **brief and easy to read.**

In your plan, make notes about the following aspects of both poems:

- the **form** of the poem and the **narrative viewpoint**
- the **key ideas** or **themes**
- how the poem is **structured**
- the **language** used in the poem.

There's no need to go into a lot of detail or to write in full sentences when planning. Use **key words and phrases** that will jog your memory when you look back at the plan. Make a note of the line references of quotations you could use to support your answer. If the quotations are very short, you could write down the whole thing.

Structure your plan in any way you want. You could use a **bullet-pointed list, table, mind map** or any other format that you're comfortable with.

As the time available in the exam is extremely limited, don't spend lots of time planning or writing an introduction or conclusion. An introductory sentence stating which poems you'll be comparing will be enough.

Here are some examples of plans for a question comparing the character's voice in *The River God* and *My Last Duchess.*

Bullet-Pointed List

Creation of character's voice: 'The River God' and 'My Last Duchess'

- Form and viewpoint. Both first person dramatic monologues – words reveal more of their characters than they perhaps intend.
  - RG – we are the audience. Does not hide his nature from us.
  - MLD – suggests the audience is a visiting servant. Openness is chilling considering reason for servant's visit.

- Structure – rhythm and rhyme.
  Both poems use rhyme to reveal aspects of the character.
  - RG – Varies throughout to reflect unpredictable character. Full rhyme reveals lack of empathy 'clowning'/ 'drowning' and near rhyme shows his seedy character 'swimming'/ 'women'.
  - MLD – Heroic couplets used throughout and subtly push the poem on. Could suggest the Duke's speech and actions are always contrived? Compare to claim in lines 35–36.

Rhythm – different techniques, same effect.
  - RG – enjambment highlights insecurities (21–22). Flowing, unending – like the river.
  - MLD – caesura emphasises lack of remorse, 'Then all smiles stopped together.' Abrupt, cold, like the Duke.

- Language: Repetition is a key feature, used for two purposes.
  1) What they notice in others:
     - RG – Admiration of beauty: 'beautiful' (14, 16, 17, 19) – vanity of RG.
     - MLD – Despises / does not understand happiness: 'joy' (15, 21), 'smile' (43, 45, 46) – coldness of Duke.
  2) Reveals things about them:
     - RG – insecure 'will she stay' (15).
     - MLD – proud 'stoops' (34, 42, 43).

Table

Creation of character's voice		'The River God'	'My Last Duchess'
Form and viewpoint	Both 1st person monologues. Neither character hides anything from audience – no remorse.	Speaks to reader – hides nothing.	Speaks to servant – reason for visit chills us.
Structure	Rhythm – different techniques, same effect. Rhyme – different types of rhyme scheme.	Enjambment highlights insecurities (21–22). Flowing, unending – like the river. Varies throughout to reflect unpredictable character. Full rhyme reveals lack of empathy 'clowning'/'drowning' and near rhyme shows his seedy character 'swimming'/'women'.	Caesura emphasises lack of remorse 'Then all smiles stopped together.' Abrupt, cold, like the Duke. Heroic couplets used throughout and subtly push the poem on. Could suggest the Duke's speech and actions are always contrived? Compare to claim in lines 35–36.
Language	Repetition: 1) What they notice in others 2) Reveals things about themselves.	1) Admiration of beauty: 'beautiful' (14, 16, 17, 19) – vanity of RG. 2) Insecure 'will she stay' (15).	1) Despises/doesn't understand happiness: 'joy' (15, 21), 'smile' (43, 45, 46) – coldness of Duke. 2) Proud 'stoops' (34, 42, 43).

Mind Map

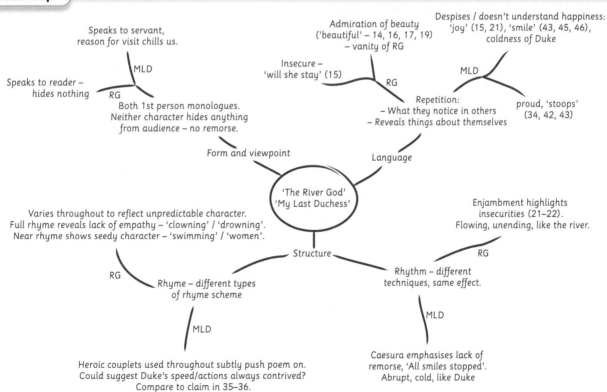

Writing a Comparative Essay

Finding Similarities and Differences

In your response to the question, you need to explain how the two poems are **similar** and how they are **different**, and **give examples** to back up your points.

As part of your revision, you could use a table like the one below to identify these similarities and differences. In each line make a brief note of the main points. Focus on identifying **interesting points of comparison** that you can explore in detail in the exam.

	Titles of poems go here	
	Similarities	Differences
Character		
Voice / viewpoint		
Themes		
Form		
Structure		
Language		
Tone		
My response		

Discourse Markers

Discourse markers are the glue that holds your answer together. They show the examiner the relationship between your ideas and arguments. Some examples of discourse markers that you could use are given below.

To show comparison	Although	Conversely	Despite
	Equally	However	In contrast
	Similarly	Whereas	While

To add information	Furthermore	In addition	In fact
	Moreover	By the same token	In connection with this

To introduce an example	For example	For instance	Specifically
	This illustrates	This is demonstrated	In relation to this

Writing a Comparative Essay

Using Quotations

You'll need to select **quotations** from the poems to support the points you make. Choose your quotations carefully, keep them short and make sure they relate to the point you're making.

Always **aim to write as much as you can about each piece of quoted text**; there should be more of your words on the answer paper than the poet's.

For each quotation think about:

- **the techniques** the writer has used
- **what** this technique contributes to our understanding of the poem
- **why** the writer may have used this technique, i.e. the writer's purpose.

Shaping Your Paragraphs

The following example outlines a format that you could use to structure a comparative paragraph, looking at how different features are used in each poem. This approach will help to make your comparative points very clear.

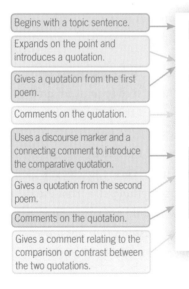

Begins with a topic sentence.

Expands on the point and introduces a quotation.

Gives a quotation from the first poem.

Comments on the quotation.

Uses a discourse marker and a connecting comment to introduce the comparative quotation.

Gives a quotation from the second poem.

Comments on the quotation.

Gives a comment relating to the comparison or contrast between the two quotations.

> The dramatic monologues 'My Last Duchess' and 'The River God' both have the abuse of power as a central theme. The Duke is so confident that his behaviour is irreproachable that he asks: 'Who'd stoop to blame / This sort of trifling?' His rhetorical question suggests that he feels we would condone his abuse of power and reveals his utter lack of understanding of the horror we feel at his actions. The use of the word 'stoops', which is repeated several times in his explanation, keeps his obsession with power at the forefront of our thoughts; as it is in his. In contrast, although the River God relishes the power he has over life and death, he seems insecure. He asks: 'Oh will she stay with me will she stay'. His power over his victim is not absolute and there is no guarantee that he will maintain his control over her. While the two characters certainly have the power over life and death in common, their faith in their power is not equal.

Tips for Writing a Comparative Essay

- Make sure you understand what you're comparing – note the key words in the question.
- Try to write a **balanced** response: don't favour one poem over the other.
- Structure your answer by taking one aspect (e.g. imagery) and exploring it in both poems.
- Start a new paragraph for each aspect you compare.
- Use **discourse markers** to signal the relationship between your ideas.
- If two aspects are significantly different, don't shy away. Highlight the fact and explain why / what difference this makes to the way you respond to the poem.
- Ensure you **maintain the comparison** throughout your answer.
- Use **quotations** to support each point you make about the poems.

Worked Sample Questions

Foundation Tier

Compare the ways that characters are presented in 'Give' and **one** other poem from 'Character and Voice'.

Remember to compare:

- the characters in the poems
- how the characters are presented.

(36 marks)

Annotation	Essay
Addresses the question.	In the 'Character and voice' poems, the writers use lots of different techniques to present the characters. 'Give' is written in the first person, so we understand exactly how the man feels about the things he does and the way people treat him. I will compare this poem with 'The Clown Punk' where we see a punk through the eyes of a man driving through a run down area.
Identifies the first poem, taken from the question.	
Makes their choice of poem clear.	
Topic sentence relating back to the first bullet point.	Both poems have central characters who are outsiders. In 'Give' the main character is a homeless man who is outside normal society as he doesn't have a job or anywhere to live and has to rely on hand outs to survive. In 'The Clown Punk' the main character is a punk. Punks were around in the 70s and dressed in an unusual way to make it clear that they did not agree with the way society was run. They wanted to be seen as outsiders.
This point could usefully be developed to help the comparison. How does the homeless man want to be seen?	
Topic sentence relating to the second bullet point.	The poets use language to present the characters. In 'Give', the man seems to be polite, he calls the person he is talking to, 'dear'. This is a colloquialism and is usually used when people are being informal, but polite. I think that he is using it because when people talk to him they think he needs to be talked to like this and they patronise him. He also uses sarcasm. At the end of the poem, he is given a cup of tea and says: 'That's big of you.' This is sarcasistic because he isn't really greatful for the tea, he wanted something else from the person. The words that describe the punk in 'The Clown Punk' are very visual. He is described using a simile, he looks 'like a basket of washing that got up/ and walked'. This suggests the punk looks scruffy because a basket of washing would contain a real jumble of clothes.
A point and a quotation to support it.	
Clear analysis of the quotation including technical vocabulary.	
Take care with your spelling.	
There is no clear comparison in this paragraph; the poems are treated as two separate things.	
Identifies patterns and changes within the poem.	The poems have different tones which help us understand the way the homeless man feels and the way the driver feels about the punk. At first, the man in 'Give' is quite polite and the tone is quite friendly as he calls people 'dear'. He says he sleeps 'under the stars' which creates a romantic tone that is surprising as it doesn't seem that unpleasant. But the tone changes as he describes what he has to do to get money. People want him to do dangerous things and he has to degrade himself and 'swallow swords, eat fire' to get money. He lists lots of things he will do and this makes him seem desperate. In the last line he is definitely unhappy. In 'The Clown Punk' the tone at first makes it seem like the driver is making fun of the punk, until he says, 'don't laugh'. This is a command and introduces the idea that we should feel sorry for the punk as he uses words like 'deflated', 'shrunken' and 'sad' to describe what
This could be supported with a quotation and comment on the effect. What effect does a final line with a sad tone have?	
This could be reworded to include a discourse marker which would make the comparison more obvious.	

the punk will look like in the future. These words all create a feeling of sadness and help us understand that the driver thinks the punk's future will not be much fun. Both of these poems have a sad tone and this makes us feel sorry for the characters.

The structure of the poems is important as it helps us understand more about how we should feel about the characters. 'The Clown Punk' is a sonnet. Sonnets are a type of poem that are usually about love. This makes me think that the poet wanted us to know that the driver likes the punk and is fond of him, he just thinks he has made bad choices. In 'Give' the structure makes me think that the poet wants us to know that the man is quite clever but that he is getting desperate and fed up. This makes us understand that the man has given up all hope for the future.

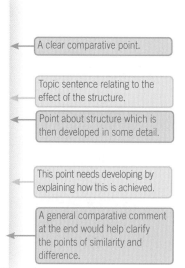

A clear comparative point.

Topic sentence relating to the effect of the structure.

Point about structure which is then developed in some detail.

This point needs developing by explaining how this is achieved.

A general comparative comment at the end would help clarify the points of similarity and difference.

Examiner's Comments

This is a C-grade response. This student has used quotations and made some comments about how the writer's techniques might affect the reader. They have commented on the ideas and themes and identified some of the similarities and differences between the poems. The structure of the response is fine, but topic sentences and discourse markers would make the relationships between the points clearer.

To achieve a C grade, you should:
- Compare the effect of language/structure/form and the way the choices the writer has made may affect the reader.
- Develop your analysis of the quotations. It might help to choose shorter quotations in some instances, as this will ensure that the detail is analysed.
- Make sure that the similarities and differences in the poems are clear and that the comparison is sustained throughout the response.

Worked Sample Questions

Compare the presentation of the character's loss in 'Casehistory: Alison (head injury)' and **one** other poem from 'Character and Voice'.

(36 marks)

Names the first poem that will be explored.

Gives the title of the poem they have chosen for comparison.

Outlines the main idea behind the response.

Good vocabulary choice.

Quotation integrated into the response.

The analysis has been sustained and this is an insightful response to the poem.

Topic sentence indicating the direction of the argument.

Close textual analysis and good use of technical language, exploring its effects.

Spelling mistake, but better to use the term and misspell it than not to include it!

This is a very small quotation but it has been explored in detail. Make your quotations earn their place in your essay.

Both 'Casehistory: Alison (head injury)' and Betjeman's elegy 'On a Portrait of a Deaf Man' engage with the effects of loss on an individual. In the monologue 'Casehistory: Alison (head injury)', U.A. Fanthorpe presents us with the voice of Alison; a woman attempting to come to terms with the loss of her memories and the promise of her future. The struggle to come to terms with loss is also explored in 'On a Portrait of a Deaf Man'. Both poems engage with the effects of the loss on an individual, and although what they have lost may be different, there are many similarities in the ways the effects of the loss are depicted.

In 'Casehistory' we are presented with a character who is unsure of what she has lost. The opening line describes Alison looking 'at her photograph' suggesting that she will be reminiscing, but the riddle-like declaration: 'I would like to have known / My husband's wife' makes Alison's separation from her past clear. The use of the conditional in the statement creates a wistful tone that lacks any anger; perhaps her lack of memories is a blessing here as it is difficult to mourn something you have no recollection of. In contrast, the voice of the poem 'Portrait' is very clear about what he has lost. The opening description of a 'kind old face' is affectionate and familiar. This may account for the more direct way that the loss is addressed in this poem.

In both poems contrast helps establish the feelings of loss. The contrast between Alison 'enmeshed in comforting fat' and 'her delicate angles' in the photograph is highlighted by the caesura between the two juxtaposed descriptions, emphasising the negativity of the first, reinforcing the idea of loss. In 'Portrait' enjambement is used to link together pleasant images, for example, of 'potatoes in their skins' with an image of a corpse with mouth 'wide to let / The London clay come in.' Here, as in 'Casehistory', the structure highlights the difference between the past and present, although the image of the present is much more graphic in 'Portrait' and suggests anger at the situation.

Repetition in stanzas 4–6 of 'Casehistory' emphasises what Alison has lost and its significance. Alison's frequent use of the word 'smiles' could suggest that she envies the physical ability to smile, or perhaps that she grieves for her previous life where she had much to smile about. In 'Portrait' the repetition serves a different purpose; the word 'likes' is repeated to link father to son and highlight the closeness of their relationship as well as acting as a bridge between the pleasant and unpleasant images.

Both poems have a very regular structure, but this has been used to different effect in each case. The regular rhythm and lack of rhyme in 'Casehistory' give the poem a considered air. Conversely, the metre and full rhyme scheme of 'Portrait' create a tone in conflict with the content, linking together images of a smiling, 'wise' man with that of a body with 'maggots in his eyes'. This reinforces the idea that the character in the poem has not come to terms with his loss and cannot separate the two different images of his father in his own mind.

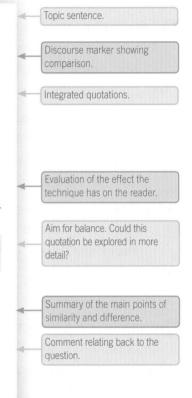

Topic sentence.

Discourse marker showing comparison.

Integrated quotations.

The isolation of the final line and it's foregrounding in the opening stanza creates pathos, as we see Alison's resignation. Her use of the third person shows us how she sees the girl in the photo as a different person. As this is the last line it suggests that she feels no hope of returning to her former self. 'Portrait' also ends with a single line: 'I only see decay', which is bleak and final, and has a similar effect of removing any hope of seeing change in the future.

Evaluation of the effect the technique has on the reader.

Aim for balance. Could this quotation be explored in more detail?

In conclusion, both 'Casehistory' and 'Portrait' use language and structure to highlight the characters' experience of loss and it is mainly in their response to it that there is significant difference. While Alison is resigned to her loss and lacks anger behind her words the voice in 'Portrait' seems unable to see the positive aspects of the past without calling up unpleasant images, creating anger which is evident in his words.

Summary of the main points of similarity and difference.

Comment relating back to the question.

Examiner's Comments

This is an A*-grade response as it is exploratory and analytical. Quotations are well-chosen and have been analysed in detail to support the insightful comments. The structure of the response makes the comparison clear and spelling, punctuation and grammar are mostly accurate.

To achieve an A* grade you should:
- Include insightful comments and interpretations.
- Provide an evaluative comparison of the ideas, meanings, techniques, language, structure and form, and the effects of these elements on the reader.

Exam Practice Questions

Foundation Tier

1 We respond differently to different characters. Compare the way we respond to the main character in 'My Last Duchess' and **one** other poem from 'Character and Voice'. Remember to compare:
- the characters we are responding to
- how our response is shaped in the poems. *(36 marks)*

2 Compare the ways that writers explore imagination in 'Brendon Gallacher' and **one** other poem from 'Character and Voice'. Remember to compare:
- who uses their imagination
- how imagination is presented in the poems. *(36 marks)*

3 Some memories are happy and some sad. Compare the way characters respond to their memories in 'On a Portrait of a Deaf Man' and **one** other poem from 'Character and Voice'. Remember to compare:
- what the memories are
- how the characters respond to them. *(36 marks)*

Higher Tier

1 Compare how personal identity is explored in 'Checking Out Me History' and **one** other poem from 'Character and Voice'. *(36 marks)*

2 We feel more sympathy for some characters than others. Compare your response to the character in 'Medusa' and **one** other poem from 'Character and Voice'. *(36 marks)*

3 Compare how a character's voice is created in 'Singh Song!' and **one** other poem from 'Character and Voice'. *(36 marks)*

Answers

These answers are only intended as a starting point and suggest 'obvious' comparisons. The tables show the main points of comparison. Try to come up with your own ideas too, then pick four or five points of comparison and refer to the poems to find examples you can analyse in detail.

Foundation Tier

1. You might compare *My Last Duchess* with *Medusa* or *Ozymandias*.

My Last Duchess	First person narrative. Repetition highlights what he is concerned with. Abuses his power. No remorse for what he has done. Who he is talking to is important. Caesura draws our attention to key moments. Last word of the poem is significant.
Medusa	First person narrative. Enjoys her power. Repetition and ambiguity suggest she is not in control of herself. Uses negative language to describe herself. Her language varies between menace and insecurity.
Ozymandias	Abuses his power. The statue is a metaphor. Anonymous narrator creates distance. The (now ambiguous) words on the statue show his arrogance and the face of the statue shows cruelty.

2. You might compare *Brendon Gallacher* with The *Hunchback in the Park* or *On a Portrait of a Deaf Man*.

Brendon Gallacher	Repetition and possessive pronouns make it clear how important Brendon was. Mother's need for facts and inability to imagine caused the narrator to lose Brendon forever. The poem has a wistful tone.
The Hunchback in the Park	All of the characters use their imaginations to escape from their lives and to give them what they need. For the narrator, even the park doesn't exist when he isn't in it. The truant boys create tigers, reflecting their strength, and the hunchback creates an ideal companion, who is his opposite. Lack of punctuation reflects freedom of imagination.
On a Portrait of a Deaf Man	Graphic images reveal how clearly the narrator imagines what is happening to his father. The language he uses to describe the images is straightforward and uncomplicated. The pleasant and unpleasant images are juxtaposed showing how hard it is for him to think about his father without imagining what is happening to his body.

3. You might compare *On a Portrait of a Deaf Man* with *Casehistory: Alison (head injury)* or *Horse Whisperer*.

On a Portrait of a Deaf Man	The narrator recalls lots of happy memories of his father. Repetition links father and son. Each memory becomes tied to an image of death or decay. The change in tone reflects the narrator's emotions. Rhyme and rhythm are at odds with the content.
Casehistory: Alison (head injury)	Alison looks back on her memories with wonder. Mix of personal pronouns show her confusion. She doesn't have any 'true' memories and has to be reminded of the same things every day and envies her former ability to retain memory of her father's death. Enjambment is used to highlight previous grace and current clumsiness. The language is very matter-of-fact, reflecting a lack of anger.
Horse Whisperer	Detailed descriptions show pride in his memory of his usefulness. Repetition reflects anger at the difference between past and present. The tone of the poem changes to anger when he remembers the way he was treated by the people he used to work for. Memories of the horses are vivid and sensory showing his affinity with them.

Higher Tier

1. You might compare *Checking Out Me History* with *My Last Duchess* or *The Clown Punk*.

Checking Out Me History	Use of non-Standard English and free verse suggests rebellion and also reflects aspects that contribute to identity. Repeated references to pain, injury and blindness suggest the importance of knowing your own history. Contrast is used to highlight the importance of some figures and knowledge and the irrelevance of others. Passivity contrasted with taking control (last stanza) shows the need to create your own identity. The final word is significant.
My Last Duchess	Duke defines himself by his possessions, title and the power he has over others. In contrast, his wife's identity is created by her marriage to him and by maintaining a chaste demeanour – things expected of women at the time Browning was writing. Her refusal to conform to expectations (maintaining her own identity) and to reinforce his personal identity ultimately led to her death.
The Clown Punk	Disrupted iambic pentameter and rhyme reflect the punk's non-conformist attitude. Words associated with images / art remind us his appearance is a creation. His appearance is the result of choices made in youth that he will carry with him into old age. Others judge him by his appearance and behaviours. Is his identity more than skin deep?

2. You might compare *Medusa* with *My Last Duchess* or *Les Grands Seigneurs*.

Medusa	She is destructive and violent but we feel she has been driven to it. In the myth, the head of snakes is a punishment; do we feel she is being punished enough? The tone of the poem varies from insecurity to threat, she is both pathetic and dangerous. Her husband is not an innocent victim. Tragedy is foreshadowed. What is the effect of the ambiguous last line?
My Last Duchess	Overuse of possessive pronouns shows his self-obsession and desire for control. Places an extremely high value on objects and status. Descriptions of his wife create sympathy for her. Rhetorical question shows us that he expects us to condone his behaviour. The word he uses to describe his aim in marrying again is significant. The rhyme and enjambment reflect the relentlessness of his moving on to another wife.
Les Grands Seigneurs	Words associated with fairy tales suggest her previous experiences gave her false expectations. The balance of the poem is weighted in favour of the past – she is reliving her 'glory days'. Her identity is entirely built around her relationships with men. Passive tense when describing her marriage suggests a lack of power as does the list she uses to describe herself. But, as she enjoyed the power she had over others it is difficult to feel too much sympathy.

3. You might compare *Singh Song!* with *Checking Out Me History* or *The River God*.

Singh Song!	The first person narrative gives us insight into personal thoughts, hopes and dreams. The use of idiolect is very personal and forces us to read the poem in his 'voice'. The rhythm and rhyme in the poem reflect his character. Even the customers' complaints are presented in his voice and are structurally separated from the rest of the poem – it is his perception of these comments that we focus on. We see how he perceives others and reacts to their expectations.
Checking Out Me History	The first person narrative focuses our attention on the things that are important to the narrator. Use of dialect makes the poem personal and reminds us of the character's heritage. Imagery, repetition, rhyme and rhythm highlight key people, ideas and events. The rebellious nature of the Caribbean figures sets up our expectation of his rebellion.
The River God	First person narrative lets us hear the character's voice. Defensive tone in first line. Repetition shows both insecurities and what is important to him. Tone of justification – thinks he has done nothing wrong. Rhyme is used to reflect his unpredictable nature and to link contrasting images suggesting his lack of empathy. Language to describe the rule-breakers is negative. Seedy personality suggested by the way he describes women.

Quick Test Answers

Example answers have been provided for the quick tests however they are intended as guidance only; wherever possible, try to think of other comments and examples you could give in response to the questions.

Pages 4–5

1. The title links the punk's outward appearance to that of a clown; both are visually distinctive but clowns are sad, solitary beings whose pathetic antics we laugh at. The punk's appearance and behaviour are designed to create fear but the addition of 'clown' suggests that it's not entirely effective. The phrase also reminds us of the description of the punk as the 'town clown' (line 2); he is something of a joke in the local community.
2. The car and the people inside it are representative of middle class culture and this is what the punk movement rebelled against. The punk's position outside the car symbolises his position as an outsider to conventional attitudes, dress and behaviour.
3. 'deflated', 'shrunken', 'daubed' and 'sad'.
4. 'Indelible ink' cannot be washed away, and refers to the permanence of the punk's tattoos. The idea of the windscreen wipers washing away the punk's image is a direct contrast to this and suggests the insignificance of the punk to the people in the car; his image can easily be erased from their minds, despite the 'indelible ink'.

Pages 6–7

1. They emphasise the lack of relevance of his education to his life and culture. The references also remind us that our sense of personal identity begins in childhood. In colonised countries children were educated in English in the history of their colonisers, distancing them from their own heritage.
2. They link them to light and brightness. This is significant as the voice in the poem is seeking enlightenment about his history and culture. Knowing more about his roots will help counteract the 'blindness' that he has about his own history.
3. With references to injury and blindness.
4. They show the voice in the poem taking control. He is rebelling and wants to fill in the gaps in his knowledge. The lack of punctuation at the end of the poem reflects the idea that his quest to find out about his culture is unfinished.

Pages 8–9

1. Modern medicine and veterinary methods.
2. Admiration: 'shimmering', 'tender', 'stately' and 'trusted'; Contrast with: 'snorted', 'restless', 'reared' and 'revolved'.
3. 'I joined the stampede,/ with others of my kind', shows us that this experience is happening to other whisperers. Although the voice we hear is unique, the message is not.

Pages 10–11

1. The first person account encourages us to feel sympathy as we understand the emotions behind her actions. We also feel sympathy for her as she was once young and beautiful but now has a negative view of herself. Our knowledge of the myth helps us see the snakes as a curse and we also know that in the myth Medusa is slain, so we assume that she will not survive this conflict.
2. The ambiguous last line could be seen as a final pathetic plea as the woman realises what she has become or it could be a threat against the man. We are not sure if the woman is a victim or aggressor.
3. 'Greek God' is a clichéd description of a handsome man. It also links in with the extended metaphor that runs throughout the poem, linking the woman to the image of Medusa and her husband as her destroyer, Perseus.

Pages 12–13

1. He uses contrasting images of comfort and threat to describe her.
2. It helps create an intimate, romantic tone which reflects the content of the section where the young couple dream together.
3. Singh is a name traditionally given to all Sikh boys and the title also reflects the shopkeeper's melodic accent and intonation. The pun reflects the light humour that is present throughout the poem.
4. It creates the feeling that there are a large number of people speaking to him this way, and that it is a regular occurrence.

Pages 14–15

1. Loss and mourning.
2. She might have created him out of loneliness, or to live a life that she romanticises, or as a way of understanding the work her father does – perhaps to feel closer to him.
3. The day Brendon is lost to her the weather is bleak. This is an example of pathetic fallacy and emphasises how important he was to her and how significant losing him is.
4. She senses his importance to her daughter. She might be being judgemental as the girl may have told her 'colourful' things about him, but this is unlikely as her father is a Communist Party worker and would help families like Brendon's.

Pages 16–17

1. Could be a challenge to the idea that the homeless could change their situation if they wanted to.
2. The reference to 'making a scene' in the first stanza could be seen as patronising as young children are often accused of this. The colloquial 'dear' as a form of address could also be seen as patronising. Perhaps the man is mimicking the way he is addressed by those who attempt to help him. In the final stanza there is more evidence; what the man wants is change, but he is given tea, which he neither wants nor appreciates.
3. 'I'm on the street, under the stars' has a romantic feel. The two contrasting images are linked by the use of alliteration and this highlights the difference between our perceptions and the reality of the situation.
4. It could be interpreted as a literal representation of the act of begging, or it could suggest that the man is at the end of his tether and can't take any more. The last sentence could then be seen as a final desperate plea for help.

Pages 18–19

1. That her ideas about marriage were naive.
2. It is ironic; she was once in a position of power and played with the affections of the men who pursued her but now she is the plaything who must try to please her husband.
3. The first three stanzas have longer lines and a slower pace, which reflects her dream-like reminiscences. The final stanza describes her present situation and has shorter lines, which reflect her anger and frustration at being reduced to a plaything.
4. No, they were sometimes arrogant and 'strutting', her 'worst of times' and her 'monkey-men'. Hyperbole might suggest she saw them as faintly ridiculous.

Pages 20–21

1. The poem is set in a vague 'antique land' to make it clear that Ozymandias's accomplishments belong in the past. The place where the statue is found has no name as there is nothing where Ozymandias's great city once stood. All his achievements have now been forgotten. We only know of the statue third hand, which further distances us from Ozymandias and his power.

2. That it is fleeting. We only know of the statue third hand, and neither Ozymandias nor the empire he created remains. The only evidence we have of his former power is the statue which was the creation of an artist.

3. The description of his 'frown' and 'sneer', the contempt with which the artist views him and the arrogance of the self-given title 'king of kings'.

4. They use oxymoron to emphasise the irony of the wrecked statue. This, along with the alliteration that draws our attention to the barren landscape, contributes to the sad tone.

Pages 22–23

1. The poem flows from one line to the next, moving on as the Duke is moving on with his next marriage.

2. Hearing the Duchess's fate from the Duke's mouth emphasises his coldness and lack of remorse. It is shocking to us that he sees no shame in telling the servant. He assumes his behaviour will be condoned, but in fact we see both her and his behaviour clearly and are horrified by his actions.

3. The repetition of 'stoops'/'stooping' in lines 34–43 highlights the Duke's obsession with power and his unwillingness to lose face. He would rather kill his wife than discuss his feelings with her. The repetition of 'smiles'/'smiled' in lines 43–46 shows his fixation on his wife and his obsession with her behaviour.

4. To emphasise the fact that the murder of his wife does not affect his conscience. She is now totally under his control and is no more than an object to boast about. Like Neptune in the statue he moves on to describe, the Duke strives to tame and control anything beautiful or rare.

Pages 24–25

1. Defensive, as though the River God is responding to criticisms he has heard people make about him.

2. In mythology gods often fall in love with human women and take them away from their lives by force without any thought for the consequences. These gods are powerful but also cruel, vengeful and wistful.

3. 'Waiting for me to smooth and wash away the fear' seems like a gentle image at first, but in fact describes the River God washing the life away from his victim and may also reflect her face becoming bloated with water. It shows us that he is unable or unwilling to see the true consequences of his actions.

4. The threat in the last line of the poem removes any trace of sympathy we may have had for the River God and reminds us that he is dangerous, jealous and vengeful.

Pages 26–27

1. Although the hunchback is mocked by the young boys, he understands that they are not intentionally cruel; they are 'as innocent as strawberries'. His ability to see their behaviour for what it is makes him appear admirable. His creation of a companion for himself makes him seem god-like and powerful. While the poem contains lots of references to locks and chains, the hunchback is never chained or restricted in any way.

2. The narrator's descriptions of the boys are full of noise and movement and show their lack of restraint and their willingness to embrace their imaginations. The descriptions also show us the narrator's isolation as he is clearly not a part of their world.

3. It suggests the hunchback is god-like as he creates her in the same way Eve was created. It also shows us that he values beauty and in making her straight we see that he does not see this quality in himself; she is all that he is not. This adds to the melancholic tone of the poem.

Pages 28–29

1. No – although the friend notices all the details of 'Melia's changed appearance and seems to be taken in by them, the repetition of 'ruin'/'ruined' throughout the poem reminds us of the true cost of 'Melia's finery.

2. It suggests this is not an isolated or unusual occurrence; this fate is shared by other women. This makes it clear that there are very few options open to women in her position if they wanted to change their lives.

3. The caesura in the final line of the poem draws our attention to 'Melia's closing words, which echo what she says in every other stanza. However, her unrefined language shows that in reality there has been very little change in her – she is still the same girl underneath. Alternatively, it could suggest that she is unwilling to change herself and is an act of defiance against the sacrifice she has made.

4. Her use of the indefinite pronoun 'one', her description of her friend as a 'raw country girl' and her friend's description of her 'strut'.

Pages 30–31

1. It suggests that what follows has been recorded and now forms part of Alison's notes – her casehistory. It also reminds us that all her memories have been lost and can only be pieced back together with the help of others.

2. Alison defines herself in terms of her relationships to others and in relation to her past achievements. She defines her present self in comparison to what she once was, not on its own merits. The description of Alison as a younger girl shows a future full of promise; the fragility of our identities is shown by how quickly Alison has lost all of that.

3. The finality and matter-of-fact tone of the last line creates pathos. It is a sentiment echoed from earlier in the poem and it reminds us of all Alison was and has lost.

Pages 32–33

1. It introduces the idea of the contrast between the man as he was and as he is now. The clothes that he is wearing fit 'loosely' and reflect his interests and personality and this contrasts to the shroud that fits 'closely' and seems constrictive and anonymous. It also gently introduces the fact that he is dead.

2. The opening line describes his face as 'kind'. He does not react badly when he can't hear his son speak, merely smiles. The seventh stanza refers to friends, shaking hands and wanting to say goodbye.

3. It is a direct address to God. It has an accusatory tone which is unambiguous and leaves us with a stark final image of the reality of death.

Glossary of Key Words

Alliteration – repetition of a sound at the beginning of words.

Autobiographical – based on the writer's life.

Ballad – a poem that tells a story. May have a repeated refrain, or chorus.

Biblical – relating to the Bible.

Caesura – a pause in a line of poetry. Usually in the middle of a line but sometimes at the start (initial) or the end (terminal).

Colloquialism – informal language; the sort of language used in conversation. May include dialect words or phrases (colloquial).

Constraint – limitation or restriction.

Creole – a spoken language combining elements of European and non-European languages.

Dialect – words or phrases particular to a region or area.

Dramatic duologue – a poem where two voices are heard, often revealing aspects of their characters and details of events leading up to the current situation.

Dramatic monologue – a poem where one person's voice is heard, often revealing aspects of their character, details of the situation and the character of the person they are speaking to.

Elegy – a poem of mourning. May also refer to a poem that reflects on death and passing time in a melancholy mood (elegiac).

Empathy – understanding someone else's feelings.

Emphatic – forcible, strong or clear.

End-stopped – the end of a sentence or clause coincides with the end of a line of poetry (the opposite of enjambment).

Enjambment – when a clause or sentence runs from one line of poetry to another, undisturbed by punctuation.

Enlightenment – understanding.

Eurocentric – focusing on European culture and/or history.

Explicit – clear.

Extended metaphor – the continued use of a metaphor for a length of time, sometimes over the entire length of a poem (see **metaphor**).

First person – a narrative viewpoint where the narrator is involved and refers to 'I' or 'me'.

Free verse – poetry that doesn't conform to any particular form or associated structure.

Futility – without hope of success (futile).

Half rhyme – an 'imperfect' or near rhyme.

Hyperbole – an exaggeration.

Iambic pentameter – a line that contains five iambs (an iamb contains one unstressed and one stressed syllable). Close in rhythm to natural speech.

Idiolect – features of speech unique to an individual.

Imagery – a collection of devices (including metaphor, simile, personification, synecdoche and onomatopoeia) which use language to create vivid visual descriptions.

Incantatory – as though reciting a charm or spell.

Irony – the tension created through the opposition of a literal meaning and an underlying meaning.

Juxtaposition – the placing of (often contrasting) words or phrases next to each other.

Melancholic – sad.

Metaphor – a form of imagery where one thing is said to be another, suggesting similarities between the two.

Monosyllabic – using one syllable.

Naive – a person without experience or wisdom. May imply innocence.

Nostalgia – longing for the past (nostalgic).

Oxymoron – the use of words which have contrasting meanings in order to emphasise one meaning e.g. 'a deafening silence'.

Pathetic fallacy – attributing feelings to non-human things, especially the weather. (From 'pathos' – 'to feel'.)

Pathos – evoking feelings of pity or sadness.

Personification – a form of imagery that gives animals, ideas or inanimate objects human qualities.

Philosophical – calm, detached and reasonable reflection.

Possessive pronoun – a word that shows ownership: 'my', 'mine', 'our', 'their', 'his', 'hers'.

Present tense – the form of a verb describing an action happening at the present time.

Rhyming couplet – two consecutive rhyming lines.

Satirical – the use of sarcasm, irony or ridicule to mock.

Semantic field – a group of words with similar associations.

Sensory – appealing to the senses or using the senses to create vivid descriptions.

Sentimental – concerned with tender or nostalgic feelings.

Sibilance – repetition of 's' or 'z' sounds.

Simile – a direct comparison of one thing to another, using the words 'as', 'like' or 'than'.

Sonnet – a poem, often a love poem, consisting of fourteen lines.

Standard English – the form of English normally used in formal writing and taught to non-native speakers. Standard English can be spoken with an accent.

Stanza – a group of lines in a poem that may have a shared meaning, metre or rhyme scheme.

Synecdoche – a device where a part is substituted for the whole, or vice versa, e.g. referring to a policeman as 'the law'.

Talisman – an object or charm thought to have magical powers and to offer protection.

Third person – a narrative viewpoint where the narrator is uninvolved and people are referred to as 'he', 'she', 'they', etc.

Unambiguous – clear in meaning.